Autobiography of an Air Force Cold War Warrior

Charles Ballew

Published by BookLocker.com, Inc., Bradenton, Florida,
U.S.A.

Printed on acid-free paper.

If you give any type of medical, legal or professional
advice, you must also include a disclaimer. You can find
examples of these online using your favorite search
engine. Most professional websites that offer advice
have these types of disclaimers.

BookLocker.com, Inc.
2015

First Edition

TABLE OF CONTENTS

CHAPTER 1: KEELSER AFB, MISSISSIPPI AND GOODFELLOW AFB, TEXAS .. 1

CHAPTER 2: 6913TH RSM BREMERHAVEN GERMANY 7

CHAPTER 3: 6917TH SECURITY GROUP SAN VITO DEI NORMANNI AIR
STATION, BRINDISI, ITALY 25

CHAPTER 4: 6922ND SECURITY GROUP CLARK AIR BASE, PHILIPPINES ... 51

CHAPTER 5: 6921ST SECURITY WING MISAWA AIR BASE, JAPAN 109

CHAPTER 6: 6993 SECURITY SQUADRON, KELLY AFB SAN ANTONIO,
TEXAS 165

CHAPTER 7: 6921ST SECURITY WING (72-74) 6920TH SECURITY
GROUP (74-75) MISAWA AIR BASE, JAPAN 177

CHAPTER 8: 6993RD SECURITY SQUADRONKELLY AFB SAN ANTONIO,
TEXAS 209

CHAPTER 9: 6920TH SECURITY WING AND ELECTRONIC SECURITY
GROUP MISAWA AB, JAPAN 219

CHAPTER 10: 6950TH ELECTRONIC SECURITY GROUP RAF
CHICKSANDS, ENGLAND 237

CHAPTER 11: 6920TH ELECTRONIC SECURITY GROUP MISAWA AB,
JAPAN 265

CHAPTER 12: DET 2 693RD ELECTRONIC SECURITY WING AND DET 2
6950TH ELECTRONIC SECURITY GROUP 279

CHAPTER 13: AEROSPACE DATA FACILITY, DET-3 HEADQUARTERS
SPACE SYSTEMS DIVISION BUCKLEY AFB AURORA, COLORADO 331

PROLOGUE

When I entered the Morse and Non-Morse Intercept Operator courses at Keesler AFB, Mississippi and Goodfellow AFB, Texas the Instructors told us that we were the top 1/2 of one percent of the Air Force's enlisted recruits. I was impressed with that knowledge until after I had been to my first four overseas tours. I worked a 4 Swing, 4 Mid, 4 Day shift schedule with a 72 break before starting the shift cycle all over again. I spent 1965 to 1985 working this type of shift work schedule. In 1985 I started working a different shift schedule. It was a 12 hour shift schedule (4 Nights 9pm to 9am, 4 days off and 4 Days 9am to 9pm). I worked as a Non-Morse Intercept Operator and Supervisor my entire 26 years and really enjoyed my duty obligations at the USAFSS and ESC operational facilities that I was assigned to. At the end of each set for shift cycles I was always ready to party hard, travel and visit different places in the country I was stationed in. I didn't think of myself as being part of such an elite organization, because it seemed to me that I was basically being paid to actually see different parts of this world. From 1965 to 1972 most of my off-duty time was spent partying at as many bars and clubs as I could find. Luckily I had a good supervisor on Trick 4 at Misawa AB, Japan that supported me when my drinking habit was out of control during my off-duty hours. Several Article 15 Non-Judicial punishments, loss of rank and correctional facility time later his support actually paved the way for my drinking alcohol in a responsible manner.

After my retirement from the Air Force I retired in my home town and went to work as a Government Contractor at Naval Subase Bangor. I had nothing in common with my co-workers and people I went to high school with. It seemed like the majority of them went to work at the local Naval Shipyard and a lot of them never really traveled that far from home. I missed my co-workers and friends I had worked with throughout my career in the Air Force. Because I had a need to see my old friends again I flew to England in 2000 to attend the RAF Chicksands reunion and visit to Edzell, Scotland, visiting and partying with friends.

Sadly both RAF Chicksands and RAF Edzell closed down their operations and our presence were no longer needed.

I took a road trip across the northern part of the United States in 2002 for the main reason of visiting ex Air force friends in Washington, Idaho, Montana, North Dakota, Minnesota, Illinois, Indiana, New York, Massachusetts and Maryland. When I received an e-mail from Helen Henderson inviting me to the USAFSS Misawa Reunion in Chattanooga, Tennessee, I was thrilled at the possibility of meeting up with the USAFSS Vets that I worked and partied with. I attended and met up with Wayne Babb at the Chattanooga Misawa Reunion along with many other members I hadn't seen in years. In 2005 I attended a mini reunion in Misawa, Japan with friends that had retired in Misawa. Ran the Bars in AP Alley for the last time and I nearly cried when I departed, knowing that I would probably never get a chance to visit Misawa again. Wayne Babb had written several books since he retired and he pushed me into writing my own book. He pushed the right buttons and this book is finally completed. This is my first attempt at writing a book. I hope everyone enjoys reading it. I have been to five Misawa Project Reunions since the one at Chattanooga, Tennessee, several San Antonio, Texas Freedom Through Vigilance Association (FTVA)gatherings and look forward to many more. I feel right at home when attending these treasured gatherings.

**Charlie Ballew
Bremerton, Washington**

Chapter 1: KEELSER AFB, MISSISSIPPI AND GOODFELLOW AFB, TEXAS

February to August 1965

Students at Keesler AFB: Nick (Philadelphia, PA), Jim (Dayton, OH)

Patrick (Detroit, MI), Marty (Boston, MA), Paul (St Paul, MN), Ron (St Cloud, MN)

I left Lackland AFB, San Antonio, Texas in late January 1965. The trip to my first technical school at Keesler AFB, Biloxi, Mississippi was by train. I was assigned to the 3380th Technical School Squadron and my barracks was located in what the base called the Triangle Area. My training school was the Intercept Preparatory Course (AQR29222). In laymen's term I was in training to be a Manual Morse Operator. We soon found out another term everyone used ...Ditty-Bop. On our first day of training the instructor told us that we were selected into the upper one and a half or two percent of the Air Force. I really never understood that perception. Technical School at Keesler AFB was a real pain in the butt for me. We marched to and from school and I was selected for K.P. duty three times during my training at Keesler AFB. In addition, we had room inspections during the week and on Saturday mornings. Since I seemed to continually fail the weekly room inspections, I was given an additional duty, mowing the grass and pulling weeds in the rose garden that was located in front of our orderly room.

We students were confined to the base during our first week. So, when we were finally allowed to get our town passes, we were more than ready to get away from the base. When I walked out of the base gate and into the Biloxi, Mississippi environment, I faced a new reality that I never experienced before. Two of the students I was going to school with and went to town with for the first time were African Americans. They were both from towns in the northern part of the states. We got on the bus that was going to Gulfport and sat in the front part of the bus. The bus driver turned and said to me "You can sit up front, but those two blacks have to sit in the back of the bus". Wow, what an embarrassing situation. We all got off the bus and decided to just see Biloxi. But everywhere we turned we faced the same situations. The restaurants were segregated, the drinking fountains were segregated and I think the toilets were also segregated. We went back on base and I don't think those two guys ever left the base until they were eventually transferred. I went to town on several other occasions and frequented a couple of the bars outside the gate. At that time, Biloxi, to me was a cesspool. I didn't like most of the local people I met and I didn't like how they treated me personally. The two highlights of my tour at Keesler AFB were when we went to the Marti Gras in New Orleans and visited Pensacola, Florida.

Half way through the training course, I heard they were looking for volunteers for the Printer Systems School located at Goodfellow AFB, Texas and I immediately volunteered. People say to never to volunteer for anything, but in this case, it was one of the smartest things I ever did in the Air Force. I was accepted and received my orders and was biting at the bit to get the hell out of Keesler AFB, Biloxi and the state of Mississippi. Those of us that had been selected for the new school went to the Airmen's Club the night before we were to leave.

While I was ordering a drink at the bar a girl came up and asked me if I wanted to dance. I said sure before turning around to meet her. I was surprised when I faced her. Both of her arms were deformed. They were half the length they should have been. She was very pretty and had a slender figure. I danced several dances with her because I felt sorry for her. I know that feeling is wrong, but it was the feeling I had. I found out later from the guys, that she was at the club just about every night and she loved to party. I was pretty much soused when I arrived back at the barracks.

As I was walking by the orderly room on my way to my room I decided to leave the Triangle Area with a going away present. I pulled up a bunch of the roses in front of the orderly room. I packed up my things and took a taxi to the train station and waited for the rest of the guys that were also going to Goodfellow AFB. We left early the next morning and as I was riding the train to Houston, I pictured the horrified look on the TSgt's face when he saw what was left of his precious garden in front of the orderly room.

We arrived at Goodfellow AFB, Texas on a Sunday. We were checked into the first floor of an open-bay styled barracks. It was immediately evident that the daily regime on this base was 180 degrees opposite that of Keesler AFB. No K.P., no marching to class and no dorm inspections (The First Sergeant did a weekly inspection, but left us notes telling us what needed to be done). We were told by other people attending the classes ahead of us that if we didn't keep the place neat and clean we would eventually be having mandatory inspections. So our class leader democratically set up a cleaning schedule for all. It was great. This base was run by the U.S. Air Force Security Service (USAFSS) and Biloxi was run by Air Training Command (ATC). I swore not to have anything to do with the ATC as long as I was in the Air Force. I felt the same way about SAC too.

The school we attended at Good fellow AFB was the Non-Morse Intercept Operator Course (ABK29232). Our classes were from noon until 6 PM. What a great set up. We were able to party at night and get enough sleep before our classes each day. One of the students I became friends with bought an old Studebaker that had a black primer paint job. I think he only paid two hundred dollars for the car. Anyway, his name was Nick and he was from South Philadelphia. I thought of him as a real women's man. He seemed to know everything there was to know about the opposite sex. He was in total shock when he found out that I had never been to bed with a woman. From that day on he tried his damnedest to line me up with some of the local girls. When it came down to having a date with one of the local girls he would line up for me, I always chickened out.

The four hot spots in San Angelo during that time were McIntire's drive-in and another drive-in Cafe on Beauregard Avenue, the Jet drive-in theater and Lake

Nasworthy (we called it Lake Nasty water). There was another place that we frequented, but not very often. I think the locals called the place the Green Door. On a Friday night during the 4th of July weekend in 1965, Nick, Ron, Pat and I went to Whiskey City on the county line and bought some beer, wine, whiskey, ice and some mixers. We proceeded out to the park at Lake Nasworthy and I had my first experience with Thunderbird Wine. I drank the wine like it was water. I even stated that it didn't have any effect on me. Right!

When I came to, I was lying in the back of Nick's car and it was still dark out. I got the shit scared out of me when I noticed faces peering in the car windows at me. I sat up and looked around. There were a bunch of bars and clubs on this dirt road which I never seen before. There was loud music coming from everywhere. When I climbed out of the car, one of the kids (which had been paid to guard the car) told me where my friends were at. One of the other kids kept pulling on my shirt sleeve and telling me his sister was a virgin and that he could arrange for me to go to bed with her for short-time. I kept saying to myself "Where the Hell am I". As I started to walk through the door of the bar that all my friends were at, Ron was walking out. I asked Ron where the hell we were and he said that we were in Ciudad Acuña, Mexico.

We joined the others who all had girls sitting on their laps and having a good old time. Nick ordered me a beer and as light-headed as I was from the wine, I forced myself to drink the beer (very slowly). There was a dancer on the floor that would dance up to each individual and we were supposed to pull a string and part of her outfit would drop off. This was done until she had no clothing at all. One of the girls sat on my lap and asked me to buy her a drink. I did and the next thing I knew she was whispering in my ear for me to go short time with her. I said no at first, but gave in later. Before I headed out the door with her, Nick stopped me and asked for my wallet and watch. He gave me the money I needed and said he would give me my things back after I got back. Like I said, he was wise to this type of lifestyle.

I slept most of the way back to San Angelo. Actually, Nick stopped the car half way to San Angelo and we all slept for a few hours. Because of that escapade in Mexico, I ended up being inflicted with crabs. Of course everyone thought it was funny as hell and of course all were wise in the ways of getting rid of the pesky devils. Nick told me of a sure cure. Shave all the hair off one side of my genital area, set fire to the other side and when the crabs scurried from the fire, you attempted to stab them with an ice pick. I went to the base clinic and was scared stiff. I swore that I would never go to bed with a prostitute again.

The instructors at our school had us fill out a dream sheet of where we wanted to be assigned after graduating from this school. We were told that RAF Kirknewton, Scotland and Bremerhaven, Germany were in the process of closing down and that we would not be selected for either one. I chose both of them anyway. The Instructors were correct about RAF Kirknewton, but were wrong about Bremerhaven. Eight members of the class including me were selected for Bremerhaven, Germany.

Chapter 2: 6913TH RSM
BREMERHAVEN GERMANY
1965 - 1966

I arrived at Frankfurt Main International Airport, West Germany, after a very long flight. It was very early in the morning when the plane touched down. Looking out the plane window, during the taxi run to the offload ramp, I noticed that it was raining and very overcast. I found out later that it rains just as much in Germany as it does in the Pacific Northwest. After passing through customs, I found out that the Duty Train taking me and the rest of us to Bremerhaven weren't leaving Frankfurt until midnight. So, all day long we (Ron, Pat, Nick and I) walked around the downtown area of Frankfurt doing some sightseeing. We were stopped four times by different peddlers within an about an hour. They were trying to sell us very expensive watches at the cheapest prices ever (right!). They all were very persistent. A fifth peddler stopped us and that's when Pat made the statement that he had just bought a watch he was wearing from another guy just down the street. Talk about one irate German, he took off down the street as if he was going to really tear into the guy that presumably sold Pat the watch. At sunset we started hitting the bars. I had never previously drunk any type of foreign beer. The first German beer I drank was called Lowenbrau. The beer was not like the beer that was exported to the U.S., its alcohol content was much more. I wasn't feeling the cold at all on the way to the train station. At the train station we got some bratwurst and french-fries at one of the many vendors. I thought that was the bratwursts were the best I had ever eaten. I slept great for about four hours on the Duty Train going north. About 4 or 5 am the train stopped at this station, which to this day I have no idea as to what town it was, and we asked one of the workers on the platform how long the train was going to be stopped there. All we got was a shrug and the German phrase that translated to "I don't Understand". We decided to take a chance and head for the main part of the train station and get something to eat. On our way back we noticed our train was leaving. We ran like hell to catch it, but our efforts were in vain. Talk about a sinking feeling. Right in the middle of Germany, God only knew where, didn't know the language, what a predicament. As we stood there, looking into the dark night, our train came back into view. We found out later that the train had changed tracks and got hooked to another pulling engine. Yes, we were very lucky.

Bremerhaven was mainly an Army transportation base. The entire Air Force contingency took up two old red brick Luftwaffe barracks. I think the Navy had three barracks and the rest of the base was all Army. After I processed into the 6913th Radio Squadron, Mobile (RSM) I found that only Pat and I were on the same operational flight. The flight was called "Able Flight" and their logo was "Mox-Nix" (Means Nothing). The Operations Building was within walking distance from our barracks. As you entered the operations building there was a picture of Johnny Cash and a write up about how he was a 292X1 Morse Intercept Operator. He was stationed at another U.S. Air Force Security

Service (USAFSS) unit in Germany. I was not aware that Johnny Cash was in the USAFSS until that time. You can see the operations building in the distance in these pictures

The 6913th RSM Operations Building

I was historically a very shy person and making friends fast was not like me. Of course this changed the longer I was in the Air Force. There was a clique on Able Flight that everyone considered the most looked up to and envied. I was determined to be part of this clique, but was not going to make it obvious that I was attempting this feat. My key to this attempt was a member of the clique that was my on-the-job trainer. He treated me like dirt (how Jeeps are normally treated) for about a month. While at work I found out in a hurry where to tune one of my R-390 receivers to (1440 KHz Radio Luxembourg). Don't get me wrong, I still tried to accomplish my assigned duties at work. This building was the only operations building that I worked in that had windows. They were double windows that with the glass panes painted black. We used them as refrigerators during the winter months. Our antenna system was a rhombic antenna system. Almost every one of my assignments after Bremerhaven used the AN/FLR-9 circular arrayed antenna system.

My trainer and others played jeep tricks on me at work, continually harassing me and telling me that I wasn't going to hack it as an X2 (Printer Systems Specialist). I kept telling myself to be cool and eventually he and others would tire of the silly games. Both on and off duty I felt very alone and feared I was never going to be part of this group of Able Flight guys. On a night after a last day watch, I took an Army bus to the outskirts of Bremerhaven and then an electric trolley-car to the town center. From there I walked across a bridge to one of our organization's hangouts. A stand bar everyone called "Otto's" which was near the Post Exchange (PX). The PX was not on base but in the downtown Bremerhaven area. Otto's and a bunch of bars on and near the Rickmers Strasse and Lessing Strasse areas were where everyone seemed to hang out at. Anyway, I was sitting at the bar having a quite drink and the Able Flight in-crowd was having a grand old time dancing, drinking, making out with some local German girls, in the booths and dark shadows of Otto's. After three mixed drinks I was about to leave Otto's and head for the bars over on the Rickmers Strasse and Lessing Strasse areas. That's when the guy that was training me at work approached me and invited me to join him and the others. Wow - Now I was part of the in-crowd, was the thought that raced through my mind. I was asked if I wanted to be a member of the "Mox-Nix" club. You bet, was my automatic answer. But there was a catch, yes, I had to be initiated. Of course there was no problem with this. Several of the "Mox-Nix" Club members pulled a few German Mark bills from their wallets and laid the money in the middle of the table we were sitting at and said that I could have the money on the table if I could successfully complete the initiation. I was starting to have second thoughts, but those thoughts were shoved aside for the chance to be part of the gang. Five shot glasses were set in front of me. First, a half a shot of a cheap German clear brew called "Korn" was poured into the five shot glasses. Then a half a shot of another German brew called Ratzeputz.

Ratzeputz

I was to drink the contents of all five shot glasses in rapid succession (called shooting your drinks). As I was reaching for the first shot glass, one of the guys stopped me and told me that they were going to make it easy for me. All I had to do was shoot three of the five shot glasses and no problem with barfing and I could still have the money. Again, there was apprehension, but there was no stopping me now. I shot the contents of the first shot glass and immediately reached for the second shot glass. As I downed the contents of the second shot I felt this agonizing flash of pain in my head, the inside of my mouth and an immediate swelling of my lips. My entire head was reeling and seemed on fire. I ran to the men's room, vomiting as I ran. I spent a good 15 minutes hugging the toilet. During all my agony, I could hear the laughter of these so-called elite Able Flight members. After cleaning myself up, I entered back into the Otto's main bar area, very embarrassed and pissed off. One of the guys tried giving me the German Marks along with a statement "you can still have the money" and then someone lit the contents of the remaining shot glasses. I looked at the bright blue flames, didn't take the money and departed Otto's.

I had decided to walk off my misery on the way to the other bars in the Rickmers Strasse and Lessing Strasse areas. My walk was longer that I thought it was. The winter night was very cold and it was snowing. Both the cold night air and the snowflakes hitting my face felt good. Most of the bars on Rickmers and Lessing Strasse areas were busy. Most of the military personnel from the base frequented this area of bars. I was looking for a small quite place, where there were very few G.I.'s. I finally found a quiet, dimly lit bar that fit the mood I was in. The bar consisted of six bar stools and three booths, all were empty. I must have set in the bar about 45 minutes brooding over what had happened earlier and nursing mixed rum and Cokes. The Lady behind the bar didn't seem too interested in me except for making sure my drinks were refilled. After about the fifth refill, she started talking with me. What was my name, where was I from in the states, etc., etc. Her name was Ingrid and she looked to be in her mid-twenties. The lighting in Bars is usually so dim that it's hard to tell how old some of the women were. She turned out to be 31 years old, 10 years my elder. If the night started off rotten, it sure ended up great. I spent the rest of my break time with her. She showed me around Bremerhaven, went out to eat and went to the cinema. She had previously lived with someone that was in the Army for about two years. Now she wanted to move back to her hometown of Munich, Germany. She moved two months after I met her and I was sad to see her go.

The Lessing Strasse area had some wild places. The Bars I ended up frequenting most often were the "Blue Angel", "Red Baron", "Rio Rita", "Columbia", "Lido", "Babylon" and a other bars I don't remember the names of. After a couple of months, I was accepted as a pretty good guy, I guess. But, I never did officially join the Able Flight's Mox Nix club. I sure didn't need them to have a great time, I was doing just fine on my own.

After a guy named Ron (which was assigned to another flight) and I had arrived at Bremerhaven, he made friends with a German national guy and his girlfriend. The German guy's name was Gerd and he volunteered to be our guide to several social events outside Bremerhaven. Gerd took us to both Hamburg and Bremen to enjoy the night life. He even knew where all the houses of ill-repute or brothels were. Gerd took Ron and I to this one brothel in Bremerhaven named "The House of Four". It was a three story brick apartment building. There were several steps leading to the front door. As we were ushered into the building, the inside hallway was carpeted and fancy silk like curtains hung in front of all the windows and there were several beautiful nude paintings of women. We were taken into this parlor which consisted of about seven love seats, and a half horseshoe style bar. Behind the bar and on the wall was a huge painting of a nude lady laying on her side. In the parlor there were several young women, all wearing slinky nightgowns or negligees. The first evening we went to this place we choked on the cost of staying the night with one of these women. $50.00 was way above our heads. I didn't have any allotments taken out of my paycheck and I cleared $43.00 every two weeks.

After a very heavy snowfall in late December 1965, I was trying out my Head slalom skis in front of our barracks. I was approached by my Able Flight commander. He inquired if I had ever skied competitively. I told him that I had not, and I had only skied off and on throughout my high school years. He then asked me if I would be interested in representing the 6913th RSM at the USAFE Ski Championships that was going to be held at Garmisch-Partenkirchen, Germany. Without hesitation, I said "Yes". In January 1966 I received permissive TDY orders to the USAFE Ski Championships. There were four of us representing the Air Force from Bremerhaven. One of the guys went with the Lieutenant, who was driving to Garmisch and a guy whose first name was Doug and I caught a train at the Bremerhaven Haupt Bahnhof train station which took us to Garmisch-Partenkirchen via Frankfurt.

We were checked into the Eibsee Hotel in Garmisch-Partenkirchen. I think it cost us a couple of dollars a night. The Eibsee Hotel was overlooking a beautiful lake and was at the base of the Zugspitz, which was an awesome mountain shooting straight up into the clouds. Its summit and lookout facilities could be reached by taking a cable car to the top of the Zugspitz. I think the town of Garmisch seemed to be mainly set up for tourist. All the homes and buildings of the town had steep roofs and murals painted on the walls and there were a lot of souvenir shops. There was a fast moving stream running through the town which added to the alpine atmosphere. I was entered into three events, the Giant Slalom, Team Relay and the Cross Country race. I finished next to last on the giant slalom race and do not remember how bad we did on the Team Relay race. The last event I was entered in was the cross country race. We had been drinking most of the night/morning before and I turned out to be the only one from our base that showed up for the race. I had a slight problem though; I was to have checked out a pair of cross country skis for this race the day before. You guessed it, I didn't get them. I showed up for the race with my slalom skis, still a bit drunk and hardly any sleep. When I trudged up to the starting gate, the official laughed and asked me what the hell I was doing. I told him not to worry his little head about it and told him to just start my time and I proceeded with the race. Out of all the entrants that were entered into the cross country race I placed last. Not bad for a racer to finish the course on slalom skis. I did have a few blisters on my feet after the race. At the award ceremonies we were all having a good time eating and drinking and I was thinking about doing this again the next year if I could swing it. After all the awards were given out, the announcement came that a special award was to be given that year. When I was asked to come up on stage and receive the award, I was embarrassed and confused as to why they were giving me this award. While standing in front of everyone, the master of ceremonies read out my special accomplishment. Basically, he said that while under the influence of alcohol I was the only person ever known to complete this cross country course with slalom skis instead of cross country skis. I was given a tube of ointment to treat my blisters, a real nice wool sweater, and some souvenir pins. I was again embarrassed when I got a resounding applause.

USAFE Ski Tournament at Garmisch

We left Garmisch-Partenkirchen the next morning for Munich where we were to transfer to another train. The train for Bremerhaven wasn't supposed to leave until the late afternoon, so we had a lot of time on our hands. While we were eating at one of the station's bratwurst stands, a huge crowd entered the train station all dressed up like in the Marti Gras that is held in New Orleans every year. As the crowd came by we were grabbed and urged to come along and party with them. I didn't want to, but the guy I was with did. We found out this big party was called the Fasching Carnival and it starts annually on January 7th and ends on Ash Wednesday throughout all of Germany. Since the lieutenant took our skis, boots and some of our gear back to Bremerhaven with him and all we had was our backpacks, we decided to go and party for a little while. Well, we missed the train out that afternoon and didn't leave until the next morning. What worried me was that we were supposed to be already back the day we left

Munich. We both knew we were probably in trouble, but both of us also thought whatever punishment we got was worth the great time we had with these crazy people. After arriving back at our base, we found that the lieutenant had already signed us in and nothing was said to us about arriving back at base late.

One evening, after a last *(1) day watch, Pat and I went bar hopping down in the Lessing Strasse area. After about three hours, we were in the bar called the Blue Angel. We were sitting at the bar minding our own business, when out of the corner of my eye, I noticed the biggest man I had ever seen walking through the door. After getting a good look at him, I noticed that he seemed to be mad at the world. He looked around the bar and then his eyes locked onto us. I immediately acted like I hadn't noticed him. He walked up behind Pat and me and put his huge hands on our shoulders. His hand seemed to cover my whole top part of my back. He asked Pat if I was a friend of his. I answered before Pat did, "Yes, of course I was a good friend of Pats". Pat bought him a drink and introduced this giant to me. Everyone called him Tarzan. Pat had drunk with him on previous occasions. I found out later that he had served time in prison for killing some German seaman with his bare hands in a fight. Yes sir, if I ever needed someone on my side in a fight, this was the guy to have. He was a very likable person, but my gut told me that I would not want to make him mad. I also was told not to play the "Sink the Bismarck" song that was in all the juke boxes wherever Americans hung out at. Tarzan hated that song and he had been seen knocking over one of these juke boxes while that song was being played. I only played the song at the bowling alley on base.

*(1) The US Air Force Security Service (USAFSS) main work schedule was 4 Swings (3-11pm), 24 hours off, 4 Mids (11pm-7am), 24 hours off, 4 Days (7am-3pm), 72 hours off and then the cycle was repeated.

In March 1966, the Air Force personnel of the 6913th RSM were notified that the Air Force part of operations was closing down. We were told to report by flight to the base theater on a specified day. I sat in the theater watching administrative people on stage milling around and arranging papers on several tables that had been put together to make one real long table. The unit commander came right to the point and said that the selection process for who was going to the two assignments had nothing to do of how long we had been at Bremerhaven. The first name drawn would be going to RAF Chicksands, England. The next name drawn would be going to San Vito Dei Normanni Air Station, Italy. After our names were called out we were to proceed to the stage and process our change of station paper work, receive our pay (an advance pay if we wished). The colonel pressed home the point that when we walked out of the theater, we were free to do whatever we wanted to do, except don't report to our next duty station before the end of April 1966. I was one of the unlucky ones that were selected for San Vito, Italy. I had heard nothing but bad stories about that place. I had planned to stay in the barracks and bid my time in Bremerhaven, but Ron Bertram brought me some news that sounded great. Yes, Ron was also selected to go to Italy. Gerd Cooper and his girlfriend offered to drive both of us to Italy. Ron and I went to Gerd Cooper's house the next evening for supper. We told Gerd that we would cash our checks and just give the money to him, although it wasn't much. The next day Gerd showed up with a briefcase in hand and opened the briefcase and we noticed that it was filled with paper German Marks. Gerd said that this vacation was his treat and he would give the money we gave him back after we arrived at our Italian destination and there would be no arguments about it.

Prior to leaving for Italy, Gerd took us to Hamburg a couple of times. There was these areas in Hamburg they called the Reeperbahn and the St Pauli District. If you like the night life and brothels, this area was loaded with bars, nightclubs and the red light establishments. We went to the Top 10 and Star clubs both times and the first time we went to the Star Club we watched the British band which I don't recall the name of, but they were very good. During our two visits we also had a great time at the All Star and Atlantis night clubs and other bars in the area. The Beetles played at the Top 10 and Star clubs quite often in their early years. There were memorabilia of the Beetles all over the walls of the Top 10 club.

The trip to San Vito, Italy was one I will never forget. Gerd, his girlfriend, Ron and I, and our luggage were all stuffed into Gerd's German Ford. We left Bremerhaven, got on the Autobahn and the next town we stopped in was Basle, Switzerland. We stayed overnight in Basle. We spent the next four days trying to get through Switzerland. Due to spring snows some of the roads were temporarily closed. One of the towns we stayed overnight at was in Lucerne. The next morning I got up early and went out to take some pictures. The town, the lake and the surrounding mountains were an awesome sight. The lake was deep blue and you could see the clouds and mountains reflection on the water. We entered Italy via the Grand St. Bernard Tunnel, Which is one hell of a long tunnel. We stayed overnight in Milano, Italy. This City has one of the most beautiful cathedrals I have ever seen. It's located at the Piazza del Duomo which is right in the middle of Milano. Our next stop was Rome. If you ever get the chance to drive in Rome, I do not advise it. Traffic is horrendous. We stayed two nights in Rome. Saw the tourist sites in Vatican City, Via Venito, Trevi Fountain and the Spanish Steps area. The Spanish Steps area was pretty interesting, lots of great night life. Ron and I said we were going to return there sometime during our tour at San Vito.

Lake Lucerne, Switzerland

The Altare Della Patria (In honor of first King of Unified Italy)

We traveled over the Apennines Mountains on our last leg to Brindisi, Italy and the San Vito Dei Normanni Air Station. Gerd found it difficult navigating the route to Brindisi. There were very few road signs giving directions. What was on Gerd's map was one thing and where we were actually traveling was another. But we finally arrived in Brindisi and checked into the Jolly Hotel which was on the main street that started at the train station and ended at the Brindisi docks area. We spent four days at the hotel not wanting to say good-by.

Gerd gave us our American money back and wouldn't listen to our insistence that he should keep our money. We made promises that we would see each other again soon and sadly went our separate ways.

Chapter 3: 6917th SECURITY GROUP
SAN VITO DEI NORMANNI AIR STATION,
BRINDISI, ITALY
1966 - 1967

I was told prior to arriving at San Vito, that I wouldn't like the base or southern Italy. I was also told that I should always make the best of a bad situation. I did not like the base or southern Italy, but I found this out for myself and in doing so I had some enjoyable moments during my tour.

I did what was required of me at work and K.P. and tried to get away from the base on my 72 hour breaks. Yes, San Vito was one of the bases overseas that required the enlisted to pull K.P. The base was about 15 minutes from the beach along the Adriatic Sea. It almost took that long to drive to the port town of Brindisi. There was very little housing on base, only the Officers and some of the high ranking NCO's lived in on-base quarters. Everyone else that had families lived in off-base quarters. I resided in the Dog Flight Dorm on base. The Base Exchange was very small, there was a three lane bowling alley, a small movie theater, a NCO club, an Officers Club and a small box by the base gas station that they called the Airmen's Club, which was closed during most of my tour. The hub on base was the cafeteria. The fast food wasn't too bad. As you can see I had to find most of my entertainment somewhere off-base. Since Brindisi was the closest big town, you would have thought that there would have been some bars, clubs and some night life. I mean, the normal military facilities always had bars, clubs and night life outside their gates. Not Brindisi. As far as I knew there were only two places of interest in Brindisi, The end of the Appian Way next to the International Hotel and the Sailors monument adjoining the Brindisi harbor. Once a year they held a wine festival on the waterfront. There was one small restaurant that I liked. The place was called Gino's Pizzeria which was near the town square.

Brindisi Harbor, Italy

FLR-9 Antenna and San Vito operations building

San Vito Barracks with FLR-9 Antenna in the background

Soon after I arrived at San Vito, there was a bad fire in the operations building burn facility (Where we incinerated classified material). It was a mess, the walls were blackened and the floor was flooded with water. I was one of the people volunteered to clean the mess up. We had to scrub the walls with soap and water and drain the flooded floor area. During our cleanup, I was ordered to empty the dirtied soapy water that we had in buckets. Since I didn't know where to get this done, I had to ask. After arriving at the back of the operations building where the faucets were supposed to be located I was searching for the water faucets when I thought I had located the water faucet and preparing to turn on the water, I heard yelling and screaming going on and looked towards the noise. Out came a couple of NCO's yelling at me to turn the water off. I hadn't turned the water faucet on and didn't know what they were screaming at me about. Apparently while I was outside the water sprinkling system in the burn room came on. I had a very difficult time convincing my flight commander that I had nothing to do with the sprinkler system being activated.

Although they refused to say I was being punished for the burn room incident I was assigned to KP duty. I was told they always needed Airmen working K.P. duties and I was a new guy at San Vito. My KP duty was for two weeks. The chow hall was sort of segregated. Officers and NCO's were supposed to sit in one area and the lowly Airmen were to sit in another. I usually got stuck with the clipper room detail or pots and pans detail.

During Thanksgiving Day of 1966, I was working in the clipper room area. There were a lot of Air Force members that brought along their dependent families to eat at the chow hall. I was working on the receiving end of all the trays with leftover food being scraped by me into garbage cans. Several of these Air Force brats threw their leftovers at us through the receiving window of the clipper room. The guy that I was working with stated that the next kid that threw his or her food at us was going to get it but good. Sure enough, this kid threw his leftover food at us through the clipper window and my clipper room workmate reached over and grabbed him.

With help of another member in the clipper room we dragged the kid through the trays, plates and garbage and put leftover food in his hair and down his back.

After messing him up we let him go. A few minutes later, the NCOIC of the chow hall arrived with a father and his kid that we messed up. The kid's father was looking for blood, specifically ours. It didn't matter what the brat had done to us, we were going to be punished. The punishment wasn't too bad, a letter of reprimand and two more weeks at K.P. My additional two weeks were spent working the pots and pans detail.

October through April you could have considered Brindisi and the surrounding area kind of dead. May through September wasn't too bad. During May through September period Brindisi and the surrounding area was hoping with transient tourist. They were either coming in from Greece and catching the next train out or coming in by train and catching the next boat to Greece. A lot of the military servicemen from base would hang out at either the train station or the boat docks trying to pick up girls that were vacationing in Europe. These servicemen were a crafty lot, they knew the easiest way to pick up the American girls was to offer them a chance at getting a good hamburger or other American food on base.

If you were lucky enough to convince the girls to go to the base, then you would then try to convince the girls to delay their departures a day or two. If a person was to be perched upon one of the buildings on the main street of Brindisi during the summer you would have been amused at the scene of numerous servicemen working their way up and down the street, talking to the female tourists, trying their damnedest to get a date. I had spent the summer of 1966 on the beach and doing a lot of snorkeling in the Adriatic Sea.

My skin was darker than normal due to being out in the sun a lot. August of that year I had rented a Fiat Spider 850 convertible and was parked near the docks by a sidewalk cafe. I approached a couple of girls that turned out to be from Iowa. I asked them if they were interested in going out to the base and getting some good old American food. All of a sudden this woman came running up and started swinging her bag at me. She called me a dirty wop, and told me to keep away from her girls, etc., etc. Everyone at the scene got a big chuckle out of my predicament, even the local Italians. I was quite embarrassed.

After spending some time in the towns of Bari, Mesagne, Ostuni, Brindisi and villages in southern Italy I began to notice lines in some of the back streets. I found out that these lines were for local prostitutes. If you did any driving on some of the main roads throughout southern Italy during the evening hours you would have seen woman sitting around 50 gal drums that were being used for fires. The guys on base called these women Campfire Girls. My roommate Jim and I made several trips up the eastern coastline to the port city of Bari. We were told that there was a University in Bari loaded with lots of single girls. We never lucked out in picking up any of the university girls, but did find out a historical fact about an old cathedral that held some of the bones of Saint Nicholas.

There was a taxi driver that went by the name of Nino. He was a local pimp and black- marketer and heaven knows what else he was into. I had spent many hours drinking the horrible local beers with him, but never asked him to set me up with a woman until this particular one evening. I had been drinking and didn't want to go back to base. I asked Nino if he knew where I could spend the night. He took me to this house on the outskirts of town, introduced me to this lady that was wearing a bath robe and had a bad limp. I was having second thoughts and was about to change my mind when the lady pulled at my arm. I told Nino that I didn't want to spend the entire night with her. He said he would come back in about three hours and take me back to the base. The reason the lady had a limp was that she had an artificial leg attached to the knee area. She sat on the bed and removed the artificial leg. That was one of the weirdest love making episodes I ever experienced. Although she was a nice enough lady, I didn't visit her again.

I will not go into detail about the black-market business that went on in southern Italy. I will tell you this. Blue label cigarettes, Cigars, nylons, cosmetics, alcoholic beverages and Kennedy 50 cent pieces were very popular items on the black-market. Nino told me that the reason that most of the people that were into black-market activities were never caught was because at each black market transaction money was additionally collected to pay off the local policia or carabiniere. Those people that refused to pay that extra money usually ended up getting arrested and prosecuted. I heard later that Nino was killed in an automobile accident in the early seventies.

During the summer of 1966, Jim and I succeeded in convincing two tourist girls to stay over a couple of days. We took them to Oria to see the Oria Castle and the hanging monks next to the castle and a few of the local places of interest. We then were able to convince the girls to visit Pompeii, Mt Vesuvius and the Isle of Capri with us. The ruins of Pompeii were very interesting, but I chickened out on taking the cable car to the top of Mt. Vesuvius. On our hydrofoil boat ride out to the Isle of Capri we could smell the sweet fragrance of the flowers on the Isle of Capri before we even got there. The Island is highly commercialized with all kinds of shops, boutiques, restaurants and hotels. We stayed at the Roberts (or Roberto) Hotel. The hotel was expensive, but was worth the cost in the end. We ate at one of the restaurants which had several tables on a large patio enclosed with exotic flowers. To top this off, there was a full moon, the night was warm and there was a slight breeze. While we ate our meal there was a violinist strolling around the patio playing soft music. If there was a situation to make points with a lady, this was it. The following day we visited the Gardens of Augustus, Castello di Barbarossa (all 800 steps) and finally took a boat ride to the famous Blue Grotto. We stayed two nights on the Isle of Capri and then went back to Brindisi. We took the girls to the ferry, so they could continue their sightseeing trip to Corfu and Athens, Greece. We both received several post cards from the girls and I received one letter after they got back to the states. I lost their addresses and never saw or heard from them again.

Old Amphitheater at Pompeii, Italy

**Jim and the two tourist gals we hooked up with.
This was in Pompeii, Italy**

The Isle of Capri Harbor in Italy

Just north east of the base was a community called Specchiolla. This area was where the majority of the married military personnel lived in off-base quarters. Specchiolla was called "Peyton Place" by those of us that lived in the barracks. Jim was from Ohio, and almost became an ordained Catholic priest, so he said. I don't know the story of why he changed his mind, but he joined the Air Force and became what we call a party animal. I never thought I would be in the same situation as Jim, but it almost happened. I was in Brindisi one day, sitting on the steps of the End of Appian Way, which was located next to the International Hotel. A green Triumph sports car drove up and the lady in the car gave me a honk and a wave. It was one of the flight commander's wives. We talked for about 15 minutes about the weather, etc. She then asked me if I wanted to drive up the beach road and spend some time swimming. I thanked her for asking me and told her that I had other plans (I lied of course). I had heard from a few of the guys in the barracks that she was having affairs with some of the single guys.

My roommate Jim was one of those guys having a sexual relationship with a wife living in Specchiolla. I continually tried to get him to stop his periodic visits and told him that he could get into a lot of trouble if he was ever caught. I guess I wasn't too persuasive, because he continued his affair. One night after our last swing shift Jim borrowed a friend's car. Jim was seen getting into the loaned car that was parked in front of the couple's house. I was told that the husband chased Jim all the way back to the base. Jim decided not to enter the base and drove further on into Brindisi, where he finally lost the husband that was chasing him. Jim parked and locked up the car and took a taxi back to base and retrieved the car the next day. Two days later Jim was summoned to my flight commander's office. Jim ended up receiving an article 15 and was restricted to the base for 30 days. The enlisted man's wife was sent back to the states and he was rotated to another assignment right after his wife left.

We had a beach party after a last mid during the summer of 1966. There were three cases of beer taken to the beach. Only two cases were consumed. At the end of our party someone in their infinite wisdom convinced us to bury the remaining case of beer. The beer should have stayed cold until we came down for another party. We wrapped the remaining case in plastic and cardboard. Dug a hole about 2 or 3 feet deep (That was a chore all by its self) and buried the beer. We paced off the steps from a large cement block that was near an embankment on the beach. You know..., we never found that case of beer again. Either someone dug them up or we were so drunk that we didn't really know the right amount of steps or the correct area.

We had a flight trip to Rome. I went on every flight trip that was organized by our flight. We left right after our last day watch by train from Brindisi. It was an overnight train ride to Rome. We partied all night long of course. I remember quite vividly a very lumpy fluid running across the outside windows of our compartment. It was vomit from one of the guys that had stuck his head out his window and threw up. We arrived in Rome early the next morning and the first thing we did was check into our hotel. From that point on we had a choice of staying with a preprogrammed tour of the city or be on our own until the scheduled departure date and time. There were six of us that decided to face the challenges of Rome on our own. We rode on horse drawn carriages, visited some of the sights, but mainly just checked and planned out our up and coming night time adventures. We all decided on the Spanish Steps area. I don't remember all the names of the bars and clubs we went to but the first one we went to was where most of the jet-setters hung out at that time. The club celebrated different cultures around the world. Hawaii week was being celebrated at that time. We were handed flower lei's as we entered the place. We had a hell of a good time dancing and drinking the night away.

We left this place about 10 PM and hit a few other places in the area. I personally did not remember too much of what we did the remainder of the night. What I do know, is that I was rudely awakened by a crowd of people. When I got my bearing and could see what was around me I found that the six of us had ended up at the Trevi Fountain. One of the guys was fast asleep with only his underwear on. We never did find his cloths. There were several people taking pictures of us. How embarrassing. One of the onlookers gave the unfortunate drunk a shirt to wrap around his waist and then we got a taxi back to the hotel. The six of us were restricted from flight trips for the remaining of the year.

I only went to the city of Naples twice to do some partying. The guys at work said that the best time to go partying in Naples was when most of the 6th Fleet was deployed. It seems that the prices at the bars went down and there were more women available when the sailors were deployed. I went with other guys on two of our 72 hour breaks. We had fun on both occasions, but I really wasn't impressed with Naples. One of the guys told us about two famous prostitutes that were given the names "Humpty Dumpty" and "Commissary Mary" by the navy men assigned at the Navy and NATO bases. What amazed me 15 years later that these two prostitutes were still talked about by Navy and Air Force members that were stationed in southern Italy. Those two prostitutes really must have been replacements and were using the same names, but who knows.

In the spring of 1967 Ron and I requested and received permission to take a 35 day leave. Ron and I had planned this trip ever since we left Bremerhaven,

Germany. We had gathered literature, maps and train schedules of countries we had planned on visiting. We also set up a day by day itinerary of each place we were visiting along our pre-planned route. This itinerary, of course, did not work out as planned. We threw our itinerary out the window on our third stop. Prior to going on this holiday, Ron and I applied for what was called a "EURAIL PASS". This pass enabled us to get on and off the trains anywhere in Europe at our pleasure. This pass also alleviated us from purchasing train tickets at every stop. This pass saved me some money in the long run too. For emergency purposes, I made arrangements with my folks to wire money to the American Express Company in Copenhagen, Denmark which was to be about our halfway point in our trip. I packed the bare necessities into my backpack. Ron preferred to take suit cases, which he regretted later. Our first stop on our trip was Venice, Italy. We had planned to stay two days but only stayed one full day seeing the sights. We took the boat tour on the Grand Canal which took us to Piazza San Marco. While there, we visited all the sights and then took the boat trip back.

The Grand Canal in Venice

Me at the Piazza San Marco

Piazza San Marco

From what I saw of old Venice, the place was really coming apart at the seams. This was in 1967. I can't imagine what condition this place is in today. I was told later that I should have taken the tour around the outside of the city via the Giudecca Canal. We left Venice in the evening, so we could sleep on the train before arriving at our next stop in Innsbruck, Austria. This type of travel saved us from paying for room in a hotel. We arrived in Innsbruck, Austria just as the sun was rising. The surrounding snowcapped mountains lit up by the rising sun and the deep blue haze in the valley's that twisted their way down to where Innsbruck lay was a breathtaking sight. Ron and I decided not to stay the day at Innsbruck and took the next train out to Garmisch-Partenkirchen, Germany. I have regretted not visiting Innsbruck ever since. In Garmisch-Partenkirchen we checked into the Eibsee Hotel, which

I had stayed at during the USAFE Ski Championships the year before. Although it was May, Garmisch got hit by a two day snowstorm and we decided to stay there for a couple of days. I showed Ron around the town and of course hit the bars during the evenings. We both had a great time. Our next stop was Munich, which I had already visited while I was stationed in Bremerhaven, but we stayed a full day seeing the sights and of course we ate and drank at the Hofbräuhaus (this Beer Hall is something else). From Munich we traveled to Heidelberg. We took a local boat excursion on the Rhine River and looked around the town of Heidelberg, Including Heidelberg Castle. From Heidelberg we took an overnight train ride to our old stomping grounds in Bremerhaven, Germany. This is where Ron wanted to spend most of his leave time. We stayed with his cousin Gerd Cooper. I stayed three days partying with Ron and Gerd. I could not keep up with those two in drinking beer. I would get drunk and Gerd and Ron both seemed to still sober. The Germans drink beer and wine like we drink water and soda pop on an everyday basis.

Ron and I left Bremerhaven and arrived in Copenhagen, Denmark where we stayed at a youth hostel that had rooms named after World War II resistance fighters. During the school year, students related to any of the named resistance fighters got free room and board at this place. During the spring and summer months, they used the place for visiting tourists. I located the American Express office and the picked up the money that I had my folks send me. We took the harbor boat excursion that showed us the harbor sites, including the Little Mermaid. Tivoli Gardens has their grand opening each year during the month of May. A large smorgasbord is set up for all visiting Tivoli Gardens. We pigged out of course. We visited the Carlsberg Brewery.

The Little Mermaid Statue in Copenhagen, Denmark

As you enter the brewery, there are two large stone elephants holding up the entrance and the front wall foundation. Other attractions that we visited were the Amalienborg Palace (the residence of the reigning royalty). This is where they have the daily changing of the guard parade just like they have at Buckingham Palace in London. We also visited the Rosenborg Castle and several Hans Christian Anderson interest spots during the daylight hours. If I was to go back to Denmark, I would like to visit Hans Christian Anderson's home, which is located in the city of Odense, which is located on the island of Funen.

Copenhagen's night life is something else, lots of bars and night clubs. If you like to party in the Scandinavian countries, you better have a bunch of money, because it's quite expensive. After staying three days in Copenhagen, We traveled to the city of Stockholm, Sweden. This city was pretty, but we thought it was kind of dull compared to Copenhagen. So we only stayed one day and then headed back to Copenhagen where we stayed one more night.

After we arrived back in Bremerhaven, Germany, Ron got involved with another girl he previously had met and wanted me to stay a couple of more days before going on to Amsterdam.

I didn't want to wait around so I said that I would stop by Bremerhaven on my way back from London.

I saw Amsterdam by a canal tour boat which I followed up by visiting some of the places I had seen on the tour. After a day of sightseeing which included the house that Ann Frank hid away in during the German Occupation of the Netherlands, I ended up down on Canal Street. I hit a few bars and did some window shopping. Although there were prostitutes sitting behind windows in Bremerhaven, there were much more of these on Canal Street advertising their profession. I looked but didn't touch. I almost gave in at one window but chickened out.

I stayed the night in Amsterdam and took the afternoon train from Amsterdam and arrived in Brussels after the sun had set. My first worry was where I was going to stay the night. I asked the guy working at the information desk if there were any cheap hotels near the train station area. He smiled and said the best place for me to look for a place would be about nine blocks from the train station on the right side. When I arrived at what I thought was the area I was looking for there was this neon sign lit up with the words Folies Belgére. There were lots of people hanging out in front of this place and you could hear music coming from the place. I found out it was a fancy nightclub. I was too tired to see what the place was like and looked for a place to stay the night.

Folies Belgére in Brussels, Belgium

After checking into a rough looking hotel I found an eatery and had a few drinks and something to eat. I had no problem sleeping that night. All the travel was wearing me out. The next day I did a little sightseeing, visiting the Brussels Market Square and the statue of Manneken Pis. I took the train from Brussels to Ostend thinking I was going to take the ferry to England that same day but that was not to be. I met these two American girls on the train that were going to visit a town by the name of Ghent. I asked them what was so interesting about Ghent. They said they were going to visit a medieval fortress called the Castle of the Counts. So I asked the girls if they would mind if I tagged along with them. No problem, so off to the castle we went. The torturing devices that were displayed in the dungeons of the castle were something else. I was glad

I stopped in the beautiful city of Ghent and the next day I caught the ferry to Dover, England.

I checked into a Bed and Breakfast near Trafalgar Square and the Soho district in London. The owner of the Bed and Breakfast let me use her washer and dryer. So I spent the first day cleaning my cloths, watching a little television and took an afternoon siesta. I was fatigued from my previous travels, so this was a day of rest for me. The next morning at breakfast I met tall red headed guy from Switzerland. He spoke English, German and Italian with no problems, which I guess a lot the Swiss people do. Anyway, he had already been in London a week and asked if he could be of any help in locating the different sights in London. This was great. I found out that he had won a two week paid vacation to London by winning a chugging contest at the University of Geneva. He was a real nut and liked to party. He told me to just call him by his nickname "Red". We saw the sights during the day and partied at night and I was having a great time. Red gave me his address in Switzerland and told me to visit him and his family if I was ever near where he lived. He even gave me a letter of introduction in case he wasn't at home. I left England after four days, wishing I had left London and visited other places further north but I had to get back to Bremerhaven and pick up Ron.

From Bremerhaven we took the train to Barcelona, Spain and instead of going to Lisbon, Portugal (we changed our itinerary again) and decided to travel to Lucerne, Switzerland. We took the tour boat ride on the Lucerne Lake and then took another train ride to the town of Altdorf. In the town square of Altdorf I was surprised to see a statue of William Tell and his son. This is the town that William Tell supposedly shot the apple off the top of his son's head. We were running out of leave time and we needed to get back to our base so I did not try to get in contact with my new friend that I met in London. Anyway I assumed he was back with his studies at the university in Geneva.

William Tell Statue in Altdorf, Switzerland

The next stop was Milan, Italy. We stayed only one day in Milan visiting the sights and then it was off to Rome and then back to Brindisi, Italy. This was a trip that I will never forget. I guess I will always have regrets on what I should have seen or what I should have done, but at least I got to see some of Europe.

Since my tour in Bremerhaven, Germany was cut short my tour at San Vito Dei Normanni Air Station, Italy was also cut short. I received my orders to Clark Air Base Philippines while I was on leave and was eager to leave San Vito. I departed San Vito August 1967.

Chapter 4: 6922ND SECURITY GROUP
CLARK AIR BASE, PHILIPPINES
1967-1968

When I got off the plane at Clark Air Base, located in the Pampanga Province, Republic of the Philippines, the only thing I knew of this hot and humid island was from war stories that were told to me from 2-T Staff Sergeants and some Air Force old timers. I really didn't believe half of the stories I had heard, but was to find out in the coming months that everything that was related to me was all true. I read in an Air Force brochure that there was a tropical ventilation setup used in the Clark AB barracks. Tropical ventilation meant that the outside and hallway walls of the rooms in the barracks were covered with screen and adjustable louvers. I had previously assumed that it was some sort of air conditioning system. Man was I mistaken.

The 6922nd Orderly Room and barracks were set up in a triangle type setting with a patio in the center. We had a bar called the Cobra Den at one end of the building that the orderly room and chow hall was located. The Cobra Den was run by off-duty personnel in the 6922nd organization. Directly behind the barracks I was staying in was a large field and across this field was a jungle infested hill that was called Lily Hill. Lily Hill was a famous battle site during WW-II. The hill was infested with caves and tunnels and divisions of our troops battled for days trying to oust the Japanese that were entrenched in this hill. The story goes that our troops enlisted the help of the local Negritos which on the first night, without being seen or caught, took several bags of captured cobras and released them throughout the tunnels and caves. The second night, they sneaked into the sleeping areas and decapitated several Japanese soldiers. The Japanese that weren't killed woke up to this gruesome situation wondering why it hadn't been them. On the third day the remaining Japanese surrendered or committed suicide. We were told that if we saw any cobras in our triangle area to contact one of the house boys and they would take care of the cobra for us. I only saw three cobras during my tour and the house boys did indeed take care of them in a very swift manner (pole and machete).

Me on the 2nd floor of my barracks

Lily Hill behind our barracks

I didn't realize how big Clark AB really was until I started processing into the 6922nd Security Group. I was told that Clark AB was one of the largest operational military installations in the world. When you enter Clark AB via the main gate and you look far into the distance, you saw a range of lush green hills that ran north and south. These hills were on the edge of a larger range of mountains that the famous active volcano, Mount Pinatubo, was located. With a base this large, security was a big problem. Some of the incidents that occurred before and after I got to Clark AB were incredible. I was told about a brand new fire engine, fully loaded with the latest firefighting equipment, drove through the main gate with its sirens blasting. The guards at the gate waved the fire truck through because of an agreement between the base and Angeles City. After the fire was under control, the fire truck was driven to Manila where it is probably used to this day at one of the Manila fire stations. I asked co-workers why the base couldn't get their fire truck back. I was told that there were many unscrupulous laws made up just so that the United States got screwed. This particular law was a hum-dinger. If an item that was stolen and legally changed ownership more than seven times, the original owner had no legal claim to the stolen item. I imagine the thieves had seven legal transactions accomplished in no time at all.

The bank, NCO and Airmen clubs were both robbed of thousands of dollars in daylight holdups during my tour at Clark AB. The thieves brandished sawed-off shotguns and automatic weapons. I don't understand how they brought the weapons on base. There were also shooting and stabbing attacks on base, usually by outraged bar girls or friends of these girls. These attacks were mainly against G.I.'s who were leaving the Philippines without their distraught ex-girlfriends. It was no surprise that the security police force at Clark AB was so large. There were air police trucks with 50 caliber machine guns mounted above the truck cabs, horse and motorcycle units for the perimeter and airstrip areas, and of course the air police for the normal everyday duties.

A couple of the guys, that I was stationed with in Italy, wanted to head for the notorious Angeles City as soon as evening rolled around on our first day at Clark AB. I tagged along with them of course. We were going against everything that we were told by the MAC terminal personnel after landing at the Clark Air Base. They told us that we were to attend mandatory organizational meetings prior to venturing off base.

None of us wanted to wait that long. We caught the next smoker (Base Bus) which eventually ended up at the main gate of Clark Air Base. Our first unexpected experience came when we were stopped by the guards at the main gate. We found out that we were only allowed to take two packs of cigarettes off the base each day. We found out later that with a letter from our commander, we were allowed to take several cartons off base when we went on leave or if we were authorized to live in off base quarters. As I left the security of the base, we were accosted by several young kids begging for money. I always said no or just ignored them. On occasions some of the kids tossed rocks at us. I found out later that these kids purposely egged you on, hoping that you would give them the money they wanted and when they didn't get any money some of these kids got nasty. When this happened, some of the GIs retaliated by physically pushing these kids to the ground.

If that were to have happen there were people at the ready with a camera and soon after a lawsuit would more than likely be filed against you in the local court system. I guarantee you that you would have lost the case. There were several Filipinos also selling pornography (they were called bedtime story books). There were dozens of makeshift booths that sold everything from souvenirs to girls. One of the big money makers outside the main gate was exchanging our greenbacks for Pesos. You know how patriotic we Americans are...the majority of the guys I knew always got their Peso's outside the gate because you got a much better exchange rate. You had to watch your money exchanges because some of these Filipino peddlers were crooked. They sometimes would slip you counterfeit Peso's (Some bills were pretty obvious...only printed on one side of the bill). After you got by all the vendors, you ran into what seemed to be a parking lot overflowing with jeepneys *(1). There were two types of jeepneys, Regular and Special. The Special jeepney took you directly to where you were going. Regular jeepneys supposedly took a specific route through town to the market area on the far side of the town. The regular jeepneys would stop, if there were room in the jeepney, anywhere along the route for people. The Special of course was the more expensive of the two rides. There was no set rate for the specials, you had to ask and haggle at the price of your ride. I found out later that it was much safer and a wiser decision if you stuck with the specials no matter what you ended up paying.

Jeepny in front of one of the local bars

The Mad Irishman and I, being new to Angeles City, patronized the bars and clubs nearest the main gate. I couldn't get over how dirty the town was. The aroma of the open benjo ditches *(2) and the stench from inside some of the bars was sickening. After completing the obstacle course outside the main gate there lay before you two huge open fields on both sides of the road leading to MacArthur Highway that ran north to Bagio and southeast to Manila. On the left side of the open field was First Street and on the right side of the opposite open field was Fields Avenue. Both streets were lined with bars, clubs and maybe a Sari-Sari *(3) store or two.

We visited almost all the bars on both First Street and Fields Avenue that night. Between the beer and the stifling heat I wasn't able to stay the night seeking out adventures with the Mad Irishman and I went back to the security of the base. I figured that this was going to be the area I would visit on a regular basis. I found out that I was wrong of course. A lot of the 6922nd Security Group, which we were assigned, hung out in an area known as the "Dirty Dozen". This area was located on the southern side of Angeles City.

(1) Jeepney: A brightly decorated Jeep taxicab.
(2) Benjo Ditch: Open drainage/sewage ditch.
(3) Sari-Sari Store: General Store.

Two days later we attended the mandatory orientation briefing. There were several speakers from different support organizations. Throughout everyone's presentation there was a case of San Miguel beer that sat in front of the speaker's podium. The last speaker was from the base hospital. He picked, at random, 10 bottles of beer from the 24-bottle case. While doing this he said "I suppose you all have been wondering what this case of beer was doing up there". Everyone just mumbled "yea". He said that if they were to analyze the 10 bottles of beer that he had just selected, the alcohol content would vary between 3.2 percent and 36 percent. His point was, if you knew how much beer you could drink prior to arriving in the Philippines; you could not safely rely on that same amount of the San Miguel beer.

His next topic covered venereal diseases. He said that 6 out of every 10 personnel at Clark Air Base would be visiting the VD clinic at the hospital before their tour was over. Along with his speech there was a very graphic film on venereal diseases. The hospital's presentation was very informative and I said to myself that I was not going to be one of the "6 out of 10" personnel contacting the clap or any other type of venereal diseases. What an ignorant young man I was.

During the first few months at Clark AB, I was trained on my military duties at the 6922nd Security Group. Our Operations was located in Building 850. Its location was close the garbage dump, the jungle survival training school and the on-base Negrito village.

The 6922nd Operations Building and the FLR-9 Antenna

The interesting and much more exciting training I received was in the bar areas of Angeles City. The town seemed to be divided into four separate areas. Balibago: This was the main area of Angeles city nearest the base. The Block: This is where the majority of the black GIs hung out during my tour. San Francisco Street: This was an area between the Block and the Market area that consisted of nothing but *(1) short-time houses and a few Sari-Sari stores. The Dirty Dozen: This was an area on the far side of town near the town market. Balibago was mainly frequented by what we called the lower 98. Let me explain the term "Lower 98". At our technical schools and at work we were always told that we were the upper 1/2 of one percent of the Air Force. So, all other organizations were referred to as the "Lower 98 Percent" or just "Lower 98". Although the Dirty Dozen was visited by most base organizations, we felt that our organization owned the Dirty Dozen area lock, stock and barrel. This area originally consisted of 12 bars in the dirtiest part of town. This area became my home away from home for almost the duration of my tour at Clark AB.

During my first three months I witnessed two dead bodies and a hit and run incident. The first dead body was of a naked Philippine guy lying on the steps of a building just off MacArthur Highway in Balibago. He had several puncture wounds in the chest area and his genitals were completely severed. The second dead body was located in a large benjo ditch off the area we called the "Strip" in Balibago.

The hit and run incident I witnessed was one of those things that I don't think I'll ever really forget. A jeepney hit a *(2) Hammer and kept on driving. I instinctively ran to aid her. I got about half way to where she was laying when I was tackled from behind by the Mad Irishman and a *(3) Kaibigan named Ernie. Ernie was a jeepney driver that we had become good friends with during our first few months. Ernie told me not to touch or help the girl that was lying in the street. This thoroughly pissed me off and I tried to free myself from their hold on me. Ernie told me that if I was to help the girl in anyway, that I would be fully responsible for her hospital bills. I told him that he didn't know what the hell

(1) Short-Time House: A place that a prostitute took you for what we called a "Quickie".
(2) Hammer: Black GI slang for an oriental girl or woman.
(3) Kaibigan: Tagalog for friend. We called the male Filipinos "Beaks".

he was talking about and I again tried to free myself. By then several other people were telling me the same thing. Needless to say, this is another one of these laws that was aimed at the unknowing American GI it was hard to turn my back on that girl laying on the street and the entire ugly scene, but thanks to Ernie, I walked away from her. The girl actually survived the accident.

A couple of weeks later the Mad Irishman and I made a deal with Ernie. We both paid Ernie $15.00 a month to take care of our needs when we were downtown. He would take us wherever we wanted to go within the city limits. We paid him extra for trips outside of Angeles City. He made sure we were never late for work. Watched over us to make sure we didn't get in trouble while we were in town. Believe me, In the long run, that monthly payment was worth its weight in gold.

I previously stated that the Dirty Dozen was my home away from home. I was safer in the Dirty Dozen than in any other part of Angeles City. I knew every Hammer, Mama-San, Barbecue Stand worker, Sari-Sari Store worker, bread boy and jeepney driver that frequented the Dirty Dozen. Most of the bars in the Dirty Dozen were open 24 hours a day, so I would go downtown after the *(1) swing shifts, after the last mid shift, after the last two day watches and all of our three day break. I spent most of my time in the U&I, Carpet Club, Dreamers Club and the 500 Club. I spent so much time in the Dirty Dozen It seemed like a permanent fixture. If I wasn't drinking, I was sleeping or passed out somewhere. I was never hurt or robbed in the Dirty Dozen. I think if anyone tried to bother me in any way, some kaibigan would have come to my rescue. I found out from some of the other guys that hung out in this area that the Mama-Sans would have one of their girl's watch over me whenever I was sleeping. The Hammers in some of the bars made up silk banners with our squadron and our names inscribed on them and these banners were hung up on the walls and from the ceilings of the bars we frequented. We had a lot of banners in Angeles City. One of the things I liked about the Dirty Dozen was that the hammers didn't bother you that much about buying them drinks. They knew that I would buy them drinks when I felt like it. In Balibago, I was continuously bugged about buying drinks for the hammers and that didn't go over to me or most the guys I hung around with.

It was only a couple of months after arriving, that I learned about this one Filipino who hung out around the Block area. He supposedly had several degrees as a black belt in Korean style karate.

He was well known for his attacks against GIs in and around the Block area. Because of these attacks several people were hospitalized. Every time I saw him, I made sure I knew where he was and would even cross the street to avoid coming near him. One day we were in the Block at the Alabama Club, when one of the hammers that worked at the club came running into the place yelling that there was a fight going on outside. We went outside to investigate of course. Not far up the same side of the street one of our new arrivals was getting the shit kicked out of him by this crazy Filipino. The new arrival went by the name of Ivy. Ivy was trying to fight back against this idiot in and around a new construction site. There were five of us and we figured we could come to Ivy's aid and scare this crazy Filipino away. When we were about half way to them, Ivy was knocked down onto a pile of wood. Ivy grabbed a 2X4 and came up swinging. As Ivy took a swing at the Filipino's head with the 2X4, the Filipino countered with a protective lunge of his forearm. The forearm was instantly broken by Ivy's blow. But Ivy didn't stop hitting his attacker and by the time we got to them, Ivy had put the hurts to this mad man. We never saw crazy Pilipino again.

When one walked through or by side streets of Balibago, the Block and San Francisco Street, you sometimes heard the sound of "pssst, pssst". This sound came from either a hammer or a *(2) Billy-boy. Usually the hammers that had lost their *(3) badge due to venereal diseases privately solicited sex in this manner. I was told many times to watch out for myself in these instances. Some of these solicitations were a set-up for robbery or even worse, murder. Rather than going to a hotel or some other establishment these hammers and Billy-boys normally offered you oral sex.

(1) The Security Service mainly used what we referred to as a 4-4-4-3 rotating shift cycle. We worked four Swings (3-11pm), 24 hours off, four Mids (11pm - 7am), 24 hours off, four Day watches (7am - 3pm) and then three days off.

(2) Billy-Boy: A homosexual or a male Filipino dressed up as a woman.

(3) Badge: All girls working in bars and clubs in Angeles City were required to wear picture badges and I think the date of their last health inspection was stamped on the badge.

My kaibigan Ernie warned me of two locations to avoid because these areas were saturated with both un-badged hammers and Billy-boys. The first area was located at the end of Fields Avenue and the second area was a building near the Block area of Angeles City. These Billy-boys didn't just work in these two areas. I knew of two or three that worked the bars using fake badges. They always dressed up in real sexy outfits and believe it or not, there were a lot of unknowing drunk GIs that were completely taken in by these Billy-boys. I heard several wild stories of GIs getting as far as the bed in the hotel before finding out that the hammer was not of the opposite sex. Another story I heard was that a GI was receiving oral sex from what he thought was a hammer. The GI was smoking a cigarette while he was receiving this oral sex. I guess the Billy-boy told the GI, in a deep baritone voice, to throw away the cigarette. All embarrassed the GI knocked the Billy-boy away and left.

Speaking of oral sex, there was an establishment near First Street in Balibago that was call the Fire Empire. The first time I visited the place was with a bunch of guys from work and we were running the bars. This place was crazy. Just about everything about sex was in this place. Complete nudity, Blow Jobs, Short Time Sex, etc, etc. The Hammer's drinks were always doubled the normal price. Anyway, I periodically ended up buying some of these young ladies drinks when I was being entertained there.

During an evening in the Dirty Dozen, Pat, Nick, Bob and I were enjoying ourselves in the Carpet Club when the door to the club was slammed open and this massive guy walked through the door, ducking his head as he entered. We found out later that he was 6 feet 6 inches and weighed 240 pounds. He was assigned to the Red Horse Team. This team went all over the world building just about anything. I guess they are like the Navy's Sea-Bee's. None of us, including the local Filipinos, had ever seen this guy around the Dirty Dozen before. Like I said, that part of town was ours. In each front pants pocket was an unopened bottle of San Miguel beer. He was carrying and drinking a San Miguel beer and looking over the crowded bar we were sitting in. We tried to act like he didn't exist and kept on talking to each other. But, we all were keeping an eye on him. All of a sudden he bellowed in a deep voice "Is there any fucking medics in here?" The Carpet Club became so quite you could have heard a pin drop. We tried ignoring him and kept on talking. He looked at our group and walked over to us, set his beer on the bar and put his large hands on Pat's and my shoulders (I immediately thought of Tarzan in Bremerhaven Germany). He asked us what squadron we were in. We told him we were in the 6922nd. A big smile came to his face and then said that the 6922nd group was A-OK. All of us breathed a little easier after that. He told us that a bunch of medics beat the hell out of a friend of his and was told that the medics hung out in the Dirty Dozen. He was definitely sent to the wrong area of town. Anyway, we told him where the medics hung out in Balibago and he staggered out of the Carpet Club. A few minutes later we heard a bunch of yelling and screaming emanating from the front of the Carpet Club. It was our large friend again. It seems that he had stepped in a pile of horseshit when he started crossing the street in front of the club. He proceeded to the nearest two-wheeled horse- drawn calluses, lifted the horse's head up with one hand and with clenched fist of his other hand, and smashed the horse right between the eyes. The scrawny horse dropped dead on the spot and the driver of the calluses was irate as hell. While some of the local Filipinos were trying to calm the calluses driver down, we told our giant friend that if he wanted to get back to base alive, he had better come to a financial agreement with the calluses driver. He ended up paying almost $400.00 cash for that scrawny old horse. What stymied me was that I had seen my uncle hit horses in the same manner and the horses just shook their heads.

Speaking of poor animals getting killed, during my entire tour in the Philippines, I only saw two live dogs in Angeles City. I never thought much about such a menial subject and I really didn't care. The only reason I brought this subject up was that all over Angeles City there were barbecue stands (Ihaw-Ihaw Grills) that sold chicken and pork shish-kabobs. Well, for a long time I thought I was always getting and eating chicken or pork and they always were pretty tasty. Of course, I was usually under the influence of alcohol. One night I was making my rounds of the bars in the Dirty Dozen, I saw the papa-san that ran the barbecue stand in front of the U&I bar. He was butchering the hell out of a dead dog and putting strips of the dog meat on a large board. I asked the papa-san if he was actually going to cook the meet. He just smiled at me and said that if I waited a few minutes that he would have a shish-kabob ready for me. I brought this subject up several times throughout the evening and found that I had been eating dog meat periodically since arriving in the P.I. There was one food item I could not force myself to eat. It was a duck egg that the Filipinos called a Balut. I was told that the duck egg was toasted to a golden brown under some mud or caribou dung or boiled. Inside the eggs were green slimy goo and the duck embryo. You were supposed to poke a hole at one end of the egg and suck the contents out. No Way! When I first came to town I thought I kept hearing someone yelling out my last name, but soon found out they were vendors yelling "Balut".

A guy we called Pollock (because we couldn't pronounce his last name), Nick and two other guys on our flight moved into a large house in the northern part of Angeles City. Their place was about two blocks from the infamous "Fire Empire Bar". Two of the guys were shacked up with hammers, and the other two just played the field with the hammers of Angeles City. Anyway, about a week after they moved into this place, they decided to have house warming party and most of our flight was invited to attend. Pat, Reese, Bill, and myself arrived at the party and one of the guys that lived at the house made the comment "Who invited the Niggers". Pat immediately went after this asshole but Reese and Bill grabbed hold of Pat and said that they would just leave. They didn't want any problems. I think Pat was agreed to this. That was until the asshole that made the earlier comment, pulled a switchblade and told Pat that he and his nigger friends better leave if they knew what was good for them. Pat erupted like a volcano. He was a raging bull. Five of us were trying to restrain him with little success. Someone grabbed the knife from the asshole and was telling him to leave the house. In Pat's struggle to break away he grabbed one of Ron B's arms and swung him against an edge of one of the house walls. Ron B.'s arm was seriously injured. When Ron B. had been thrown aside I filled the empty gap. As I did so, I was smashed in the face by one of Pat's fists, bloodying my nose and hurting my pride. They eventually got Pat out of the house and calmed down. Me, I was pissed off as hell at Pat because of what he did to Ron B. and I didn't want to be anywhere near Pat and was feeling sorry for myself. I went to the Dirty Dozen and was trying to keep away from Pat. When I heard from one of the bar hammers that Pat was looking for me in the Dirty Dozen I snuck off to San Francisco Street. I was drinking beer at in front of a sari sari store when Pat, Reese, Bill, and a bunch of other guys, including Ron B. with his arm in a cast, came walking up to me. Pat was apologetic and he chided me about being mad at him for such a little thing like a bloody nose coming between friends. What could I say? Ron B. wasn't even pissed off at Pat. We were friends again (Who needed any enemies when I had a friend like Pat).

In northern Luzon, Benquet province was a city called Bagio. This part of Luzon was at a higher elevation and is about 10 degrees cooler all year long. The people of northern Luzon speak the Ilocano language instead of Tagalog that was spoken around Angeles City area. The City of Bagio was built on the contours of several pine tree covered hills. The city's roads wind their way throughout the city of Bagio. Located in Bagio was the U.S. military recreation center of Camp John Hay. It was mainly a resort for the military and their dependents. You could reserve a bungalow with bedrooms, kitchen and other necessities for a small fee. Anyway, The Mad Irishman, Bob O., Ken A. and I decided to spend one of our 72 hour breaks in Bagio. I was asked to rent a car from the base car rental agency and we were off to Bagio. Right outside the Clark AB main gate we turned left and then went down First Street. Half way down First Street I hit a pot hole with one of the front tires and got stuck. The pothole was so deep that the underside of that part of the car was resting on the ground. When these potholes were filled with rain water, no one could see how deep they really were. We got a jeepney driver to help pull us out of the pothole, and then we were off again. Driving north to Bagio wasn't too bad until we started driving up into the highlands. The road had a lot of curves and we had a few close calls with buses and ox drawn carts. On the drive up to Bagio all but one of us (Me) was downing mixed drinks containing Jack Daniel whiskey. Everyone except me was pretty well lit up upon arriving at our reserved bungalow.

That night we went into the main part of this hilly little town looking for action. What a dead town compared to Angeles City! Anyway, we found a place to drink and we were all having a good bullshit session when into the bar came this entourage of about 14 Filipino's. All were carrying guns of all sorts and sizes. It turned out that the main man of this group was a senator by the name of Perez. It also turned out that Senator Perez hated Americans. He bought us all a round and proceeded to tell us the evils of our United States government and the people who supported it.

Ken, being diplomatic as could be, returned the favor by buying all of them a round of drinks and politely said that we had to be going. We were all glad Pat hadn't gone ballistic on these guys. Our bodies would have made the front pages of the local and international papers if he had. Anyway, we went looking for another place and while doing so ran across a couple of hammers who were hanging out at a corner. We asked them if they knew of a good place to party at. They said that there was a place outside of town, further up in the hills, and that the club was a great place to party at. They also wanted us to take them with us. Pat and I was the least drunk at that time and he insisted on doing the driving. One of the hammers sat between Pat and Ken and the other hammer sat in back with the rest of us. On the way up this horrible windy road, Pat came around this corner and was immediately onto an old railroad bridge that had been converted for automobile traffic. Anyway, Pat missed the two tire lanes and ended upon the rail road ties that lay beneath. In doing so the car scrapped the side railing of the bridge. We came to a complete stop and tried to shove the car sideways, trying to get the tires on track. After about 30 minutes we gave up and continued across the bridge, scrapping the driver's side of the car as we went. We even lost both door handles. We arrived at this place in the hills and indeed, it turned out to be a great place. It even had the back rooms to take the hammers to.

After the sun came up, we headed down the mountain to Bagio. As drunk as we all were, we made it across the old railroad bridge without incident. We were all hungry, so we decided to go to the golf course clubhouse restaurant and eat breakfast. In the clubhouse, there were a lot of slot machines, so instead of eating breakfast, Bob wanted to gamble. While doing so, he kept dropping his coins and when attempting to pick his coins up, he would fall down. A couple of times he looked like an ostrich trying to put its head into the ground. We tried to get him to give the machines a rest and come and eat with us, but no way. Bob then disappeared towards the men's room. After he didn't return, I went looking for him. He was nowhere to be found. We did find out something though. Our car was gone. Yep, Bob had swiped the car keys somehow and took off. We all went back to the bungalow to get some sleep and hoped that Bob would show up with the car. Bob finally showed up about noontime and he had no recollection of having driven the car or where the car was. We were lucky that Bob still had the car keys in his pocket. Bob went to bed and we went looking for the car in a rented taxi. We found the car near the Burnham city park and it had a flat tire. Otherwise, the car was still operational. After changing the flat tire we went back and got Bob out of bed and we all went to some Igorot native village on the outskirts of Bagio and bought woodcarvings and other souvenirs. When we arrived back at the Clark AB barracks and everyone unloaded their stuff, I was scared to turn the car back in to the rental agency. Although we paid $50.00 deposit for any damages done, I knew that we had more than $50.00 in damage. When I drove into the parking area of the car rental place, I parked, so that the passenger side was the side that was visible to the office. I signed the car back in and the guy said that I would probably be getting my $50.00 deposit back in about a week. Yea, right! I had a message waiting for me at work to call the rental agency as soon as possible. I called and the guy was quite irate. He asked what the hell did we do to the car and did we fill out an accident report, etc, etc. I was blacklisted from ever renting a car from the rental agency on base for the rest of my tour at Clark AB. What was ironic was that I wasn't the one driving when the accident happened.

That trip to northern Luzon was not the last for me. I fell in love with the Bonuan Blue Beach and Long Beach areas just north of Dagupon City, located in the Pangasinan Province. Bonuan Blue Beach was located on the Lingayan Gulf (South China Sea). At the Bonuan Blue Beach area, there was an old Filipina and her daughter Celeste that owned and took care of these five or six beach nipa-huts. A nipa-hut was a bamboo house on stilts with a thatched roof. These huts consisted of a hammock with mosquito net, one chair, one small table with a metal pitcher and washbowl setting on it. There was an outhouse further off the beach in the sand dunes. The cost per night at that time equaled to about 25 cents in American money. The house that Celeste and her mother lived in was behind their (1) carinderas on the beach. In front of their place were a couple of picnic tables under a thatched roof to protect you from the sun. We ate all our main meals at this establishment.

(1)Carinderas: This is like a canteen, small café and small general store all together. I don't think they really called these establishments by this name up at Bonuan Blue Beach.

In back of my Blue Beach Nipa Hut in 1967

Sunset at Blue Beach in 1967

My initial trip introduced me to the fact that this area was not yet commercialized. The people seemed to be naive in the ways of the world. The main transportation in and around Dagupan City were motorcycles equipped with sidecars. They were locally called Tricycles. They were decorated in the same manner as the jeepneys. We would arrive at the Dagupan bus station and then take these tricycles out to Blue Beach. What a wild ride! The kids ran about the beach without any cloths on at all. The older girls wore just a piece of material tied about their waist and nothing covering their breasts. Several of these young fifteen or sixteen year old girls walked around selling roasted peanuts that they carried in a large woven basket. I made a lot of friends immediately as did the rest of the guys that periodically went with me on these get away trips to Blue Beach. It seemed that on every trip up, someone on the beach was getting scrapped or cut and of course sunburned. I left my first aid kit with Celeste on my first visit to Blue Beach and later brought a more extensive first aid kits with extra bandages, lotions and creams. Everyone at the Blue Beach area soon knew where to go for free first aid attention. One time we brought up a softball, bat, gloves and a couple of Frisbees and the beach area went crazy with softball games. I have never played softball where the girl participants were half naked. It was fascinating. We left the bat, gloves, balls and Frisbees there for future use and eventually brought more softball equipment to supplement the original equipment we brought up. Other items that Celeste and the local hangouts at the beach liked were American magazines of all sorts. Again, I brought them all the magazines I could get my hands on from our 6922nd dormitory areas.

On one of my 72 hour breaks at Blue Beach, I decided to take a day hike north on the beach. I walked about five miles when I came across this small fishing village. I think there were about 25 men in the water pulling on this fishing net. As I was standing there watching, some of the men beckoned me to come on in and help pull in the net. I did so and I found that pulling in one of these nets full of fish wasn't such an easy chore. One of the fishermen told me he had an outrigger and if I would like to see more of the coast, north or south, he would take me in his outrigger canoe for just two packs of American cigarettes. I told him that I would like to take him up on his offer but that I would like to wait until my next trip to Blue Beach. He then invited me to his house to have something to eat. After I met the entire family and we were eating, I saw two round-eye females walking down the path that went by the fisherman's house. As it turned out, they were both Peace Corps workers. They said that they taught at schools within that district. I ran into these two Peace Corps workers again on two other trips to this fishing village.

**Pulling in fishing net at Blue Beach
near Dagupon City**

Behind the sand dunes of Blue Beach there was a historical marker that commemorated the 8 January 1945 landing of the U.S. forces at Bonuan Blue Beach. The marker was situated in a square that was surrounded by two or three bars and one night club.

**Blue Beach Monument to 1945
US Forces Landing Site**

On another trip to Blue Beach, I took up that fisherman's offer to take me for a ride in his outrigger canoe. I gave him three packs of American cigarettes, but after the trip gave him three more packs. We traveled north along the beach areas. After about an hour I began to wonder about the seaworthiness of the outrigger we were riding in. The canoe seemed awful fragile to be out at sea. The trip took about 45 Minutes and after landing at this fishing village, I bought the fisherman and myself something to eat at this sari-sari store which seemed to be the hub of the fishing village. After walking around the village and the beach we stopped at this place that had three picnic tables. Over the picnic tables was a thatched roof. Anyway while we were having a San Miguel beer an old man from the village came and sat with us. The old man didn't speak any English, except for one phrase which he quoted to me often throughout my stay. The phrase was "Goddamn Japanese". He offered us a drink, which he called Tapuy. I think it was a rice wine. I tried it, and politely acted like I enjoyed it. It really tasted horrible.

Blue Beach Outrigger Canoe

Ride in Outrigger Canoe

Small Island and Fishing Village

Besides drinking San Miguel beer, I liked this local rum they called Tanduay Rum. The GIs called the rum TDY. A pint of TDY cost about 25 cents. I drank TDY quite often and was unaware of what was happening to me. I would be drinking with the gang when I started having loss of memory and passing out after just a few drinks. One time I passed out and the guys I was with decided to take me back to the base. On our way back to base in a jeepney, I woke up and asked where we were and where we were going. After finding out that we were headed back to base, I guess I got upset and stepped out the back of the jeepney as it was going down the road to the gate. I scrapped my knees and elbows up during the landing, and headed for Fields avenue and continued my drinking. Other incidents that occurred were falling off bar stools and ending up in places I didn't remember going to. One night after our last swing, we went to the dirty dozen and partied all night. After getting back to the barracks the next morning and was in my bed sleeping I suddenly awoke screaming out in pain. My head seemed like it was being bashed in with a baseball bat and I could hardly see anything. Anyway my house boy came running into the room to see what I was screaming about and he found me in convulsions. He told another house boy to call the emergency room for an ambulance. When I regained my senses in the hospital, I was strapped onto this gurney and I had an IV hooked up to me from a bottle of a clear liquid substance. One of the hospital staff was standing over me. His left eye was swollen and red. It turned out that while I was having these convulsions, the emergency room staff was trying to strap me down onto the gurney and while doing so my knee hit this guy in the eye. He told me that they could have been working on one of the wounded personnel that had been flown in from South Viet Nam instead tending to a town drunk. That statement hurt. If one were to visit the hospital at Clark AB, during our conflict in Viet Nam, they would have seen wounded G.I.s lined up in the hallways awaiting operations and medical treatment. Later, the doctor told me that I had alcohol poisoning. He said that like other Philippine alcoholic drinks, there were probably no rigid controls on the brewing of this Tanduay Rum. He also said that there was probably some kind of narcotic they used in making this local rum. He said it wouldn't bother me health wise if I just had them in a moderate way. I decided not to drink any off-base Rum and Coke the rest of my tour.

That was not my last visit to the hospital. The V.D. clinic at the hospital had a huge staff. You couldn't get an appointment on the weekends or holidays if you suspected that you had the clap or any other communicable disease. Normal hours were Mondays through Fridays. I nearly screamed while taking a piss at work and the crotch area of my Air Force 1505 uniform had a wet spot from my leaking in the crotch area. One of the guys at work who was wise in the ways and symptoms of V.D. gave me a prophylactic device (a rubber) and told me to cover the penis and this would stop the leakage from showing up on my pants. This occurred on a Friday night and I suffered through the weekend. I went to the hospital on Monday morning and found myself standing in line with more than a 40 some odd people. At the beginning of the line was a person telling you to milk your penis and deposit the drainage onto a slide he was holding. (What a horrible job). We then had to sit and wait for the results. The first group of names they called out was those guys whose results were negative. I was in the group that had positive results. Those who had positive results were interrogated. The room we were interrogated in had a huge card catalog library, which contained just about all the registered and unregistered hammers in town. We were to locate the card that had the information about the hammer who gave us the V.D. in this library and then a local Philippine/American medical organization would take care of the girl that was infected. A lot of times the GIs didn't know where or who they got their case of clap from. After the interrogation it was off to get treated. When my name was called out I went behind a curtain where on the floor there was painted with two footprints and on the wall there were two painted handprints. I was to put my feet on the footprints on the floor and my hands on the handprints on the wall and first lean on right foot. I received the first penicillin injection on the right side of my butt, then I then had to lean on the left foot and I was again injected with penicillin. I had to get another set of shots 10 hours later and then finally again after another 10 hours had lapsed. I was told not to drink any alcoholic beverages, coffee or soda pop for the next 30 days. I also had to attend a mandatory film on venereal diseases. The film scared the hell out of me. They showed a metal device that was inserted into the penis. While inserted in the penis a scraping apparatus was opened and the device was withdrawn scraping the inside of the penis as it was withdrawn. Tears came to my eyes and I swore that I would never let this happen to me. I found out that after a person gets the clap several times a scar tissue builds up in the urinary tract of a man's penis and that's when they have to use this torture tool to scrap the tract clear of this buildup. Five months later I caught the clap again. So learning my lesson the first time did not work out.

Pat and several other guys told me that I should buy some tetracycline. They said if I took that medication, it would ward off most venereal diseases. I thought of using it, but when Pat woke up one morning in the barracks and found his left nut was swollen and hanging just below his boxer shorts. Pat told everyone that his left nut was hanging half way to his knee (He liked to exaggerate a bit). He was admitted into the hospital and was there for three days. When we went to visit him he said that after he was admitted the doctor asked him if he had been taking tetracycline. Pat was surprised that the doctor knew what he had been doing without any other questions or doing any tests. The doctor told Pat that he was just one of many who ended up with swollen testicles due to mixing alcohol with the antibiotic medicine.

He also told pat of the dangers of acquiring medicines on the local market. He said that one person thought he was getting penicillin, but in fact was injected with wild root cream hair oil. As a result gangrene set in on his buttocks. Pat had to keep his swollen testicle on an ice pack during his stay and his kidneys had to be flushed. Pat told us that they gave him a pitcher of beer once a day. In response, we told him "yea Pat, sure they did". Anyway, I was glad I didn't take Pat's or anyone else's advice on purchasing local medications.

Jeepney drivers, as you probably already have figured out, were a raunchy breed. The majority of them were pimps for local round-eyes (European and American women) and hammers alike. There were a lot of them that robbed, killed, and would fight on the drop of a dime or Peso. Their weapons consisted of tire irons, the shift stick that was not properly secured, an assortment of knives (including the machete), and a large assortment of guns. I guess I shouldn't place such a bad reputation on all jeepney drivers. I should state that there were a lot of the jeepney drivers that committed these evil deeds.

One evening there were about seven of us off Baker Flight doing what we did best, running the bars. The first place we visited was the House of Bamboo (I think that was the name). They had strippers that were very entertaining and live sex shows (Audience participation was encouraged with these sex acts). One of the strippers completely amazed me. She had six Ping-Pong balls, 5 white and 1 black. While she was gyrating around the stage she inserted all six ping pong balls into her vagina with the black Ping-Pong ball being inserted last. She then would dance around the stage and then while doing sensuous gyrations the ping pong balls came out of her vagina. All the white Ping-Pong balls were dropped out first and then the black Ping-Pong ball dropped out last. That was some act. I could never bring myself to get involved with the live sex shows but several of the people on flight got up on the stage and did their thing. If you were sitting next to the stage and you set your beer bottle on the stage and balanced a coin on top of the beer bottle some of the strippers could and would pick up coins with their vagina. Talk about muscle control! Another stripper shoved a peeled banana up into their vagina and would dance around the stage and periodically would give a jerk and a piece of the banana would drop onto the stage. I only went to one of these shows, but it was a show I will never forget.

I was running the bars in an area we called the "Strip" in Balibago one evening. This area was a side street running parallel to MacArthur Highway that was separated by a large benjo ditch.

I was walking towards the Lemon Tree bar when this drunken GI staggered towards me and pushed me to the ground while yelling at me to stay the hell out of his way. He staggered a few more feet and entered one of the many bars on the Strip. A couple of jeepney drivers helped me to my feet and asked me if I wanted that guy wired up. I didn't understand the term "Wired Up" and asked them to explain. They both laughed and one of them said, "Do you want that asshole killed". I looked at both of them and thought to myself that they must be joking. They were not joking, they were dead serious. I told them that I didn't know the guy and even If I did know him I wouldn't have him killed over such a stupid incident. They said it would only cost me 15 Pesos, Which wasn't too much in American dollars at that time. I thanked these guys for assisting me and gave them a couple of cigarettes and walked into the Lemon Bar. This experience and the hit and run incident made me realize how little these people thought about someone's life. I also realized that if I made any enemies that my life wouldn't be worth a damn either. From that point on,

I tried my damnedest not to offend anyone, GIs and Filipinos alike.

Across the main street from the Strip was a huge place called the Shamrock Club. Every time we went to this place it was jammed packed. The draw to this place, besides the hammers, was a live band called the Chit and the Madisons. They were the best band in the area during that period of time. Chit, the lead female singer, was outstanding. I loved her exact rendition of the song "White Rabbit". I learned to try and sit with my back against the wall or a support pole in the Shamrock due to fights and the theft of wallets. When the Shamrock was crowded, which was almost always, there were some Filipinos that would rob you without your knowledge. The robber would cut the back pocket that held the wallet off the pants of a drunk that wasn't aware of his surroundings or who had a hammer sitting on his lap that was in cahoots with the robber.

Just before I left the Philippines, the Madisons Band opened their own club at the intersection of the base road and MacArthur Highway. I heard that someone tossed a grenade into the Madisons Club and there were people killed and hurt in the incident. This happened after I left the Philippines.

I was told by some of the old timer's at work that if we were downtown during an impending typhoon to stay downtown as long as I could. If I played my cards right I could get stuck downtown during the typhoon. The typhoon alerts were set up in three stages. On the third stage the base closed down everything and locked up all the base gates to all on and off traffic. Of the two typhoons that hit our part of the Philippines during 1967-68, I was only lucky enough to get caught downtown during one of these typhoons. We partied by candlelight. The only other natural disaster I went through was a hard-hitting 7.6 earthquake that hit just north of the Angeles City area during the evening of 2 August 1968. I was at the U&I bar in the Dirty Dozen area when I was knocked off the barstool I was sitting on. All the girls started crying. I grabbed two of them and told them everything was going to be ok and not to be afraid. What a brave man I was. Bar signs fell down all over the town and power was lost and again we partied by candlelight.

On an "After the last Swing " running of the bars Pat and I didn't go back to base and after we had slept away the hottest part of the day in one of the bars on Fields Avenue we continued our running of the bars. We had worked our way down to the Dirty Dozen and day had fallen to night. Neither one of us thought much about when we should head back to base and get ready for our first mid shift. At 1000 (We had to be at work at 1100) we decided that we were going to take the first mid shift off. We convinced ourselves that all we had to do is call Ken A. (our immediate supervisor) and tell him that we were going to take that night off.

We were sitting at the bar in the Carpet Club when I called work and asked for Ken A. I related to Ken that Pat and I had decided to take the night off. Ken told me that he was not authorized to give us or anyone else the night off. We had to get permission from Tech Sergeant (TSgt) Mac. I told Ken to get TSgt Mac on the phone and we would ask him for the night off. While I was waiting for TSgt Mac to come to the phone, I relayed what Ken had told me to Pat. Pat said, "Let me talk to Turkey-neck". Pat only asked him politely once and after TSgt Mac said to Pat that we had to come to work immediately Pat said "Fuck you, we are never coming back" and then slammed the phone down. I asked Pat what the hell he was doing and that we were in the shithouse now and so on. Pat told me to quit whining and enjoy the good times while they lasted. Right then and there I should have returned to base, but I didn't and we continued to have a great time. Two hours later Ken and TSgt Mac showed up at the Carpet Club. TSgt Mac sat in his car and Ken (embarrassed as hell) stuck his head through the club door and yelled at us to come back to the base. We went over to Ken and tried to convince him to come on in and have a drink with us. Ken told us that TSgt Mac was waiting in his car and wanted us to go back with them. Pat walked out the door and yelled at TSgt Mac that if he didn't get out of the Dirty Dozen immediately that he was going to kick the shit out of him. Ken and I pushed Pat back into the bar and I told Ken that we would see him the next night at work and that we were too drunk to be of any use at work anyway. They left us in the Dirty Dozen that night and we had a glorious time.

After returning to work, we both received a Letter of Reprimand and were told to report to the NCOIC of operations the following day. We reported to his office as ordered. The NCOIC of Operations didn't show up to work so his office put us to work doing odd jobs around the operations building. Our illustrious NCOIC did not report for duty that day. After he came back, he gave both Pat and I the punishment of the burning of classified materials in the operations burn room. The problem with that detail was that just days before, the chimney had collapsed and burning of the classified materials in the operations building was impossible. The unit had an alternate burn site between the huge circular arrayed antenna (AN/FLR-9) and the base garbage dump-site (the Negrito village was also located near the garbage dump). So we were ordered to work the hours of 11 am till 6 p.m. loading the burn-bags into a truck at our operations building and driving out to the alternate burn site and burn all the classified paper materials. This was to be done under the watchful eyes of an E-5 (SSgt) or higher. The first week we had someone watching us burn at all times and then it became sporadic. We even had days when no one showed up to watch us burn. On a day when it was over a hundred degrees in the shade and the humidity was also high (as usual). We were burning, when Pat said he wanted to go over to the Negrito village sari sari store and buy some cold beers. Since no one was monitoring our destruction of the classified materials I agreed with him. Later our CMSgt showed up unexpectedly and asked where the hell was the inspector that was supposed to be there when we burned. We had an inspector at all times the remaining days of our punishment. Actually, I think the CMSgt liked us. Who could complain about the hours we worked. We partied after we got off work at 7 PM and came back to base each day between 9 and 10 AM. During the remainder of my tour I occasionally ran into the Chief in and about Balibago and me and whoever I was with usually had a good bullshit session with him.

Bob O. and I were born the same date and year and since we were such good customers at the U&I Bar the mama-San decided to throw the both of us a birthday party. She told the entire bar owners in the dirty dozen and those GIs that frequented the U&I bar about the party and we invited the people we worked with, including our jeep (new) flight commander. The Mama-San and other Dirty Dozen individuals donated and cooked the food and all we had to do was pay for the drinks. Mama-San allowed us to bring our own booze if we could get it off base. Bob O. and I both drank Jim Beam and by the day of the party there were about nine bottles of Jim Beam behind the bar at the U&I. Actually Bob and I preferred Jack Daniels whiskey, but we enjoyed the bottles of Jim Beam. There was a big turn out from all corners of Angeles City. Besides making us lumpia and a pancit, the Mama-San cooked a Filipino specialty for us, barbecued dog. And her daughter gave us a silk banner with our names and the 6922nd Security Group sewn onto it. We had several of these banners hanging from bars we frequented throughout Angeles City. Our flight commander didn't last long and we thanked him for attending our party. When Bob O. and I periodically get together these days we still talk about that grand old birthday party. Bob and I still have the pictures of this birthday party to reminisce over.

Charlie & Bob's Birthday Party

Charlie's Birthday Kiss

There was a lower 98 club that we periodically went to in Balibago that was called the Pink Elephant. One of the reasons we went there was because it was air-conditioned and the other was there was a couple of good-looking hammers working there. It was a fairly large place with stage and dance floor. On one evening our personal jeepney driver (Ernie) dropped us at the Pink Elephant, parked outside and waited on us. It was a good thing that Ernie waited on us. Pat, Bob and I entered to a fairly crowded pink elephant. We found three seats together at the bar and started socializing. At one of the tables that surrounded the dance floor there was a GI with his head lying in his folded arms (dead drunk). A short while later, the guy fell off the table and landed on the floor. A GI wearing combat boots with his civvies walked toward the passed out drunk and reared back and kicked the guy in the head. Pat jumped off his barstool and yelled at the asshole, asking him why the hell he kicked this guy in the head and that he wasn't bothering anyone. The asshole asked if that guy was a friend of Pats. Pat didn't know the guy and the asshole told Pat to mind his own fucking business. At that all hell broke loose. As I stood up my head was hit with a glass or bottle and all I saw was stars. I don't really know what happened after I was hit but will relate what Pat and Bob told me. As the brawl ensued around me, a chair came crashing out through the front door window. Ernie jumped out of his jeepney and ran into the chaotic mess. He saw me crawling on the floor and proceeded to drag me out of the club. Ernie and some other jeepney driver put me into the back of Ernie's jeepney and about the same time Pat and Bob come running out of the club and jumped into the jeepney and told Ernie to get us the hell out of Balibago. I came to my senses while Ernie was taking us to the safety of the Dirty Dozen. I had one hell of a headache and a large bump on the back of my head. The mama-San in the U&I gave me some aspirin and fixed up an icepack and had one the bar girls hold it on my head. The next day we found out that the drunk that got his face kicked in was in the hospital with missing teeth and had a broken jaw. Another guy that was in the brawl had a fractured skull. I wanted to go to the hospital to find out if my head was ok, but Pat and Bob advised me against it because the base authorities were still looking for the participants of the brawl. Since my head was no longer hurting (except when I combed my hair) and the swelling had gone down, I took their advice. I never returned to the Pink Elephant.

There was a curfew imposed during my tour. We had to be back on base by 11 pm or face the wrath of our commanders. Of course a lot of us broke the curfew regulations and sneaked around Angeles City eluding the security police from base. We were ok in the Dirty Dozen and San Francisco Street areas of town but taking risks in Balibago and the Block areas. One night, Bob O, the Mad Irishman and I were in the Dreamers Bar on Fields Avenue when curfew time arrived. The Mama-San closed the curtains and locked the door and I assumed we were about to spend the night the bar. A few hours later Bob, who was sitting near the window, decided to look outside. When he pulled the curtain apart to look outside, he looked right into the face of a security policeman. The police started banging on the door and telling mama-san to open up. All three of us ran for the back door as the Mad Irishman and Bob headed out the back door, I was grabbed by one of the hammers and she told me to hide upstairs. I went upstairs with her. The area upstairs is where all the hammers slept. I heard the Mama-san tell the police that we had ran out the back door and they followed suit. I wish I had a movie of the following epic, because it seemed to me to be a movie unfolding before my eyes. There was a window above the bar that overlooked Fields Avenue and one of the dirt streets that led off Fields Avenue. When Bob and the Mad Irishman went out the back door they went down the back side of the buildings on Fields Avenue until they arrived at a cement block factory. At the factory they went over the wall and landed on some corrugated tin roofing material. In doing so they woke up the whole neighborhood including the guard dogs in the factory area. As I was looking towards where all the barking and yelling were emanating from, I saw Bob and the Mad Irishman running up Fields Avenue with three dogs nipping at their heels. They were followed by the two security policemen. At the intersection, the Mad Irishman turned left and Bob kept on running down Fields Avenue. The dogs followed the Mad Irishman, The security police split up to continue the chase of the curfew offenders. Ten minutes went by and although all I could hear was the dogs barking, I kind of figured that Bob and the Mad Irishman's attempted escape would be for not. I then saw the Mad Irishman come running towards Fields Avenue and he jumped into a benjo ditch that ran parallel to the street, and then crawled under a Jeepney that was straddling the benjo ditch. Then a security policeman came into view with the three dogs chasing him. He ran to their parked vehicle and got in and safe from the dogs. A few minutes later I saw Bob coming down the side street and he saw the dogs at the police car and turned around and headed back from where he had just come. A few minutes passed and then I saw Bob and a security policeman walking towards Fields Avenue. They put Bob in the vehicle and drove back to base. Pat crawled out of the benjo ditch and snuck back to the Dreamers Bar where we let him in. He stunk to high heaven. Mama-San took his cloths and washed them and we spent the remainder of the night at the bar. Bob refused to give out our names and received an article 15 as punishment for the curfew violation. Like I said, I wish I had that whole escapade on film.

Dreamers Bar on Fields Avenue

A few months later another after-curfew-hours incident happened to me. This time only the Irishman and I were involved. We were at the Geisha a Go-Go bar in Balibago (The bar used to be the U&I Bar in the Dirty Dozen). All the curtains were drawn and the doors were locked. The customers consisted of two Filipino men which were regulars at the bar (they would mysteriously disappear when the PC's came around on their daily rounds). The hammers said they were associated with the Huks. I didn't care as long as they didn't bother us. Anyway, we were sitting at the bar and they were sitting at a table. They were sitting with their backs to the wall, one had a 45 pistol lying on the table and the other had what looked like the old Thompson machine gun lying against the wall. The music was being played low and all was well. All at once the door got kicked open and in rushed these three Filipinos laughing up a storm. When the door got kicked open the two Filipinos sitting at the table went for their weapons and were about to open fire on the intruders and then started screaming obscenities at them for scaring the shit out of everyone. I don't know about the Mad Irishman, but I nearly did shit my pants when it happened. They were definitely drunk, but were able to temporarily fix the latch and then locked the door. One of the intruders had what looked like a brand new M-16 rifle. He asked us if we could get him some Ammunition for his M-16 rifle from the base firing range. He told us where some of the ammunition was stored and said he would make it worth our while. We told him we would think about it and get back to him. Right!

There was one area that the town patrols seem to avoid. That area was called San Francisco Street. This street was located near the market area of Angeles city. San Francisco Street was loaded with short-time houses and sari-sari stores. One evening after curfew there was five of us hiding out on San Francisco Street. We were continually being tempted by the short-time hammers to go with them to their particular place. All of us decided to have a go with this one bunch of hammers and we all proceeded with our sexual activities in separate cubicles. I was smoking a cigarette after my sexual encounter when I heard Ken scream "You fucking Bitch" and it sounded like someone or something made a thud against the wall or floor. I wrapped a towel around my waste and proceeded out my cubicle door. I was met by Pat and two others as I came out of the door. They were also wrapped at the waste in a towel. We opened the door to where Ken was located and turned on his cubicle light. Standing there over the hammer he had just slapped to the floor. Ken was standing naked as a jay bird. What stood out immediately after the light was turned on was the fact that there was blood all over Ken's mustache, mouth and chin. Yep, Ken attempted to eat some pussy and paid the price for being unaware of the hammers monthly situation. Ken yelled at us to swear to him that we would never tell anyone what had just occurred there. We all started laughing hysterically (Except Ken) and promised him that no one would ever know of this event. Right! On the very first Swing shift at work, there were banners on the walls and pamphlets with all the details of Ken's adventure being passed around to everyone on Baker flight.

If a person looked east of Angeles City you would see a single impressive mountain on the horizon. This extinct volcano rose over 1000 feet and was named Mt. Arayat. The local Filipinos called this mountain "Huk Mountain" due to the Huk gorilla forces hiding out in that region during the 50's and 60's. Well, on one very hot and humid Sunday I and another guy that was on my flight was at the Geisha a go-go bar. Ernie drove up in his jeepney and joined us. After a few cold San Miguel beers Ernie said that this would be a great day to go up to Arayat Mountain and do some swimming at one of the parks on the mountain. Some of the hammers in the bar got all excited and tried to convince us to go and take them with us. We said that we didn't have any bathing suits and everyone just laughed and said so what, we didn't need any. So we piled into Ernie's Jeepney and off we went to the mountain. Ernie took us to a recreational area that had a waterfall landing into a huge green colored pool. Ernie had brought along some inflated inner-tubes and the hammers jumped into the pool cloths and all. We threw the inner-tubes into the pool and joined the frolicking hammers. We jumped in with our only our underpants on. I didn't want to get out of the water. It was colder than I thought, but man did it feel great. While we were swimming, a group of Filipinos decked out in camouflage uniforms and armed to the teeth, strolled by the pool. They stopped and waved at us and went on. Ernie said they were probably local Huks. We goofed off for about two hours and then headed back to Angeles City. On the way back Ernie wanted to stop at the barrio he lived in and attend a cock fight. He said that the cock fights were held every Sunday in just about every town in the Philippines. We told Ernie that we needed to get into Angeles City before dark because we didn't have a barrio pass. Ernie had a barrio pass but said he would get us back to town before dark, which he did.

Mt Arayat

Mt Arayat waterfalls & pool

When the time came for me to make a decision on whether or not to re-enlist for another hitch in the Air Force or get out, my choice was to stay in for another hitch. Why? I had been stationed at bases in Germany, Italy and the Philippines during my first four-year period. While being stationed at these bases, I traveled extensively during my off-duty time and my Air Force job was challenging and interesting. One benefit that I also took into consideration was that my specific Air Force job was entitled to a hefty re-enlistment bonus which included a onetime lump sum payment plus a yearly bonus payment for every year I re-enlisted for. (I probably would have made a good Air Force recruiter at that time). To go along with my re-enlistment, I also took a Guaranteed Re-enlistment Assignment (GRA). I re-enlisted with the guarantee that I would be staying at Clark AB, Philippines for another tour. Pat and I signed all the required re-enlistment paperwork and given a day off from work. While filling out the paperwork we found out that if we were to travel through South Vietnam the same month we re-enlisted that all our pay for that month would be tax-free. So five of the new re-enlistee's, including myself, requested a one-week leave in Bangkok, Thailand, which we would fly to via Tan Son Nhut AB, South Vietnam. This enabled us to get our normal month's pay and our re-enlistment bonus free from all taxes. The next morning we reported to the conference room at the operations building for our re-enlistment ceremony. There were over 20 of us from our organization that re-enlisted with us. Pat and I had been in Angeles City all night and we both looked like hell when we showed up at the ceremony.

A couple of days later we were on a plane headed for South Vietnam. During the plane's descent into Tan Son Knut Air Base there was an immediate change in direction and speed. The plane gained altitude and the pilot announced that they were being delayed and would be in a holding pattern. When I looked out the window I noticed several big white puffs of smoke in and around the Air Base. Tan Son Nhut AB was being bombarded by some sort of rocket motor fire. After a 30-minute delay we landed and those of us that were destined for Bangkok, Thailand and other places were immediately transferred to other planes or shelters. Most of the passengers on our Bangkok bound plane were military members stationed in South Vietnam going on a hard earned R&R.

In Bangkok, our group checked into and stayed at a military R&R hotel. The first night out on the town we decided to hire a taxi driver to take us around to all the hot spots of Bangkok. He told us to call him Johnny (He probably thought we couldn't pronounce his real name). He said he could take us to the Sampheng Lane (a red light area) anytime we wanted or go to several of the night spots in the Potpong area. We wanted to check out the clubs and bars in the Potpong area. Just about everywhere Johnny took us the bar or nightclub owner would give him a small bamboo cage with what looked like a huge cockroach inside the cage. He had accumulated a bunch of these cages when he finally dropped us off at the hotel in the wee hours of the next morning. From what we gathered from Johnny, these cockroaches were partial gifts for bringing customers to their establishments. The first place we went was a big nightclub that had a local band playing. The music wasn't too bad but when the band members attempted to sing in English they really sounded bad. Since there were the 5 of us we decided on taking turns buying the rounds of drinks. I was first and ordered 5 Singha beers. We offered Johnny a drink but he said, "If Johnny Dink, Johnny gets Dunk". The Thai's definitely didn't pronounce those "R's". We were kind of surprised when they brought us five huge bottles of beer. For the rest of the night we ordered one beer and 3 glasses.

Thailand's Singha Beer

Johnny, singer from the Band, Charlie, Reese & Pat

Two of us (one of us was me) didn't like the taste of the beer and started drinking whiskey. I asked for the whiskey and coke mixed drinks the rest of the time we spent in Bangkok. No matter where we went to the bartenders denied that the whiskey was rum, the whiskey they gave me sure tasted like rum to me. The so-called whisky drink still tasted better than that Singha Beer. After midnight we asked Johnny to take us to one of Bangkok's many massage parlors. The place Johnny took us to was equipped with a bar, wall to wall carpeting and a waiting room. In the waiting room there was a beautiful girl sitting at a desk. She opened the curtains that hung along one of the walls. Behind the curtain was a long sectioned-off window. This setup reminded me of looking in at newborn babies at a hospital. Except that we were looking in at about 30 girls in skimpy white dresses with numbered red badges pinned above the right breast area. We were asked to make our selection of the girl we wanted. That was difficult since the majority of the hammers were all good-looking. I selected the hammer with number 27 and paid for the works (body massage, sex and a hot bath). I left there a very clean, refreshed and satisfied man.

A worker at the R&R hotel told us that Bangkok was called the "Venice of the East" and just about everything that happened in Bangkok included the city's waterways. During the daytime a couple of us traveled around the city acting like tourists and taking pictures. This included a trip to the renowned Bangkok floating market. Besides the boatman that controlled the outboard engine and steering at the aft end of the large canoe there was the three of us taking a very wild ride on that river. I kept expecting the boat to collide with everything that we were zipping by. They sold just about anything and everything at the floating market, even counterfeit U.S. silver coins. I bought a couple of rings and a few uncut stones at a very low price and to this day wished that I had bought a lot more than I did. But at that time I was only interested in hammers and booze. I wasn't very materialistic during that period of my life. I was smoking a cigarette while walking through part of the market when suddenly, out of nowhere, this monkey swung by the front of me snatching the cigarette out of my mouth. The monkey swung up into the canopy of the market area and then disposed of the cigarette. Was he trained to do that? I don't know, but this monkey sure scared the hell out of me. I lit up another cigarette and kept an eye out for other monkeys while I finished my shopping.

BangkokTemple of Dawn

Going up river to the floating market Floating Market in Bangkok

The third night in Bangkok, we got split up into two groups. The group of guys I was with decided to come back to the hotel early that night and get some much needed rest. I was beat from lack of sleep, being in the sun all day during our sightseeing and of course the partying during the night hours. I agreed to turn-in early. About 3am the next morning the night manager of the hotel rang our room and told us to get down to his desk right away. Pat and his group were in an altercation with some taxi drivers outside the front of the hotel. I looked out our hotel room window and saw a truckload of Thai soldiers (They might have been some sort of military police). The taxi drivers were giving the authorities their side of the story and I figured that our friend's asses were had. We went down and calmed Pat and the other guys down a bit. It seems that Pat went off on one of the taxi drivers that were loitering out front of the hotel. The taxi drivers had continually asked us for cigarettes since our arrival and Pat got fed up with their constant begging. A fight broke out between Pat and the begging taxi driver, which brought the wrath of all the taxi drivers down on Pat. Between the hotel clerk, the Thai military police and the newly arrived US Army Military Police, everyone was calmed down and we were warned that if we were involved in any more trouble of this kind that our commander would be receiving a nasty report about the incidents. We were not bothered by any of the taxi drivers that hung out in front of the hotel the rest of the time we were in Bangkok. They must have also been given a warning. Anyway the rest of our leave went without incident and we headed back to Clark AB in the Philippines ready to pass on our war stories to our co-workers and friends.

There was one more place I wanted to visit before I left the Philippines. A lot of guys at work talked about this waterfall that you had to take a dugout canoe ride to get to the falls. Since the base tour office offered this Pagsanjan Falls tour I signed up for it. The falls was located south of Manila in the Laguna Province. The dugout canoe trip up the river was insane, but well worth it after seeing the falls.

Pagsanjan Falls

Pat had already departed for his new assignment at Misawa, Japan and I was settling in and making plans for my extended stay in the Philippines. I then was given some unexpected news. I learned the hard way about thoroughly reading everything very carefully before signing any document. Thirty days into my GRA in the Philippines, I received PCS orders for Misawa,

Japan. I went to the personnel office and inquired heatedly about the pending assignment to Misawa, Japan. It was like I was talking to a wall. There was a clause in the GRA that stated that I could be transferred to another installation within the same Pacific Theater to meet the needs of the Air Force. They only guaranteed 60 days of the GRA. They couldn't transfer me to the European Theater but could transfer me within the Pacific Theater. I got royally screwed, blued and tattooed and I couldn't do a damn thing about it. The start of my next four years in the Air Force was getting off on the wrong foot with me. A month later I was headed for Misawa AB, Japan.

Chapter 5: 6921ST SECURITY WING
MISAWA AIR BASE, JAPAN
1968 - 1970

I left Clark Air Base, Philippines wearing only my Air Force 1505 summer uniforms. I traveled to Japan with two suitcases that went into the plane's luggage compartment area and I had one carry on handbag. The C-141 we were flying arrived at Tachikawa Air Base, which is located near Tokyo, Japan. This base was also right next to Yokota AB. When I departed the plane to walk to the bus that was taking the passengers to the terminal, I was met by a bitter blast of cold air. I had no winter clothing (Air Force issue or civilian issue). Talk about being unprepared. I was transported by bus from Tachikawa to Yokota Air Base where I waited for the next flight that was taking me to Misawa Air Base. I drank lots of hot coffee and tried to keep warm by huddling under one of the heating vents in the main terminal area.

I left Yokota AB on a C-130 Hercules. When departing the plane at Misawa AB I was horrified to see nothing but snow every direction I looked. Misawa Air Base is located in the northern most prefectures on the main island of Honshu. The prefecture was called Aomori-Ken. After departing the plane, like when I departed the plane at Tachikawa AB, I was again met by a bitter blast of cold air. Those of us that were assigned to the 6921st Security Wing were taken to the

Wing's orderly room, which was located on what was known at Misawa AB as the "Hill". On our bus (Blue Goose) ride to the hill, I noticed the deep build-up of snow on both sides of the road. We first passed the Base Air Police Headquarters and Correctional Facility, the road then wound ("S" Curves) by the Japanese Self Defense Air Force (JASDAF) communications building (The Mole Hole) near the end of the base air strip. Then the road straightened out until there was a "Y" in the road. Just before the "Y" intersection off the left side of the road there was a fenced in facility on top of a hill which I found out later was the Air Force Technical Applications Center (AFTAC). If you traveled the road to the right you went to the base ski lodge, golf course and the base beach. If you went left (as we did) you went by the bottom portion of the mini ski slope and then across a small bridge that spanned a small creek that ran from a small lake to a larger lake. Both lakes were frozen at that time of the year. The name of the larger lake was Lake Ogawara. Continuing up the hill there was picnic grounds on the right and then a bit further you ended the trip to the "Hill" in front of the post office or next to what used to be the "Hill" fire station. After signing in at the orderly room I found out that I was to be assigned to Trick 4. I asked "what was Trick 4"? I was told that the operational flights used the word "Trick" even though they were operational Flights at Misawa. Trick 4 was Dawg Flight. Later after talking with several old timers about the origination of the word Trick I was told that the word Trick was used by the Army and when the Air Force took over our operations the term Trick was adopted by our Air Force operators at Misawa. None of any of my other assignments used the term Trick. Pat was already assigned to Trick 3 (Charlie Flight). The orderly room personnel gave me my in-processing paperwork, issued me a U.S. Air Force arctic parka and showed me to my assigned dormitory and room that was also located on the "Hill". The dorms were long two story buildings. The only part of the outside of the first floor you could see was the top part of each room's window. Between the normal snow accumulation and snow that fell off the roof the outside of the dorms looked like something you would see in the arctic somewhere. My dormitory was Dorm 7, which was located next to the Security Wing's Chow hall. The "Hill" consisted of the 6921st orderly room, post office, small Base Exchange annex, Enlisted Member's Static Club, dormitories, a four or six lane Bowling Alley (Can't remember) and the main operations building. The "Hill" also had a huge circular arrayed antenna system (AN/FLR-9). Just about all the bases I was assigned to used this type of antenna system. I was assigned to a room of my own since I was a senior airman (E-4).

Misawa Main Gate

Road to the hill operations area

The AN/FLR-9 Antenna on the Hill Operations area

After I hastily arranged my things into my locker and dresser I proceeded to find Pat who was assigned to Trick-3, but wasn't scheduled to start work yet. After getting him out of bed he and I took the bus down to what everyone referred to as "Main Base". The bus ride from the hill to the main gate of Misawa AB took about 15 to 25 minutes (depending on weather and stops). Pat showed me around the main base area. We first went to the main Base Exchange and I browsed for items I thought of buying when I got my travel pay given to me. Our first priority was processing in with the base finance office. During my first tour at Misawa we were actually paid in Military Script which was called MPC and soon as I was to find out, the bar and club owner's downtown allowed us to exchange the MPC for Yen. The Japanese Yen rate during my first tour of duty at Misawa was 360 Yen to the American Dollar. We then followed this up by going to the main base Airman's club. I joined the Airman's club to get a few of the club's benefits (check cashing, money exchange and club entertainment). From the Airman's club we took the next bus to the main gate of the base and then walked to the off-base world of bars, clubs and hammers. All of this was for me to explore and hopefully to delight in. I was hoping I wouldn't be too disappointed in the local nightlife at Misawa after being forced to leave my great tour in the Philippines. Pat didn't think I was going to like Misawa and he personally wanted to go back to the Philippines. After leaving the main gate, there were almost immediately two alleys full of bars and clubs off to the right side of the street. This area was known as "AP alley".

I don't remember the names of all the drinking establishments in AP alley during my first tour at Misawa, but from what bars I do remember off-hand were the Rintou, Sakura, Cave, Toy's, Michi's, Trick, Rhythm (This is where I met Masako for the first time. She later ran the Metro and ended up running the Companion Bar), Top Hat, New Tokyo, Country & Western Nashville, Jacks, Jupiter, Nina's, Flamingo, Relax, and the Florence. Like the drinking establishments in the Philippines, the bar and club names changed continually through the years due to the change of owners, etc. We also referred to the downtown areas as the "Mach" which was short for the Japanese word Machi (meaning town).

Snow piled up in AP Alley

Like Angeles City in the Philippines the bars in the town of Misawa were claimed by base Air Wings, Groups, Squadrons and Detachments. It didn't take me long to find out that the 6921st Security Wing (most of the Japanese locals at that time still referred to our group as First Radio which derived from the original RSM station at Misawa) had a firm grip on most of the places in downtown Misawa. In AP Alley, the Sukura, Toy's, Trick Bar, Jupiter, Flamingo, Florence, Jacks, Companion, Nina's & the Metro were some of the main First Radio hangouts. When you departed the other end of AP alley you came out onto the main street of Misawa, which was an East – West type of street. When anyone followed this main street westward to its end, you would end up at the Misawa train station, which was located in an area that the locals called Furamaki. This street was narrow, like most Japanese town streets, and eventually during later tours at Misawa became only a one way street going east. There was a mixture of bars, clubs, restaurants, hardware stores, furniture stores, etc. up and down this street. The only bars I went to on this street were the Home Bar and Honey Club and a few others I can't remember. Just past the Honey Club there were two dirt alleys which we called Pig alley or Crumbo-Cho. These two alleys were cluttered with small wooden buildings that had 4 or 5 stools standing in front of a small bar or a couple of tables with chairs. All of these shacks had back rooms with tatami mats on the floors. I usually stopped by these alleys in keeping away from the Base's Town Patrol. I rarely ran into anyone from base when drinking there.

I would have to say that after my first night out on the town I was really disappointed to say the least. I was expecting to go to bed with a Japanese girl on the first night. Pat was right, I had hoped Misawa was going to be an enjoyable assignment and then I thought nothing but bitterness about being there. I was really feeling quite low. Another irritant was the fact that the base had imposed a curfew sometime before I had arrived there. We were not allowed to be drinking in any of the bars, snacks or clubs after midnight. I heard that the reason the base commander imposed the curfew was because someone came into the Rintou Bar and shot the place up and wounding one of the customers (Can't confirm this).

I think the biggest change in my life was the fact that I had become accustomed to the life style in the Philippines and I was expecting the same type of off-duty lifestyle at Misawa, Japan. No way! I was definitely in the midst of a different class of people and I had to face that fact and adjust to it. Since I had already been stationed in four different countries, I personally was already aware of what I thought was needed to adjust to my present situation. One of the first things I realized was that if I was going to have any chance at having a great time in Japan it was mandatory that I attempt to learn as much of the Japanese language as possible. Although most of the O-Josans (young woman –which we left out the "O' in front of Josan), in AP Alley spoke enough English to get along, most of these English speaking josans were located predominately at the American servicemen hangouts. When I ventured out into the Japanese bar world or out of town areas, very few josans, mama-sans or the Japanese patrons spoke little English, if any at all.

The one thing I was still pissed off about was the Air Force assignment transfer issue. I was attempting to adjust to my new way of life downtown, but was shaking off my Air Force duties. Specifically, I had only processed in at the base payroll office and nowhere else. I finally received a note on my room door for me to report to the first sergeant at the hill's orderly room. Since I had been out partying most of the night I figured that the First Sergeant could wait until I got some sleep. The First Sergeant caught me in my bed with a hangover after I had just a few hours' sleep. He gave me an hour to get cleaned up, get into my uniform and report to him. He was upset at me to say the least. After giving him my sob story about my assignment to Misawa, he took my story into consideration, but said I was totally in the wrong and was to complete my in processing immediately. They had no pity on me, but my punishment was just a letter of reprimand, which was put into the group's local filing system.

A couple of days before I started my first shift with Trick 4, I was walking down the main street of Misawa and came upon a car that looked like it had hit one of the telephone poles along the main drag of town and the driver was just sitting behind the steering wheel of his car. The guy looked like he had a few too many. The car must not have been going too fast because I couldn't see any damage on the front end. Anyway, one of the josans that worked at the Honey Club on the main drag came walking up and she knew the guy and she said she would help him into the Honey Club. The Honey Club had already closed up for the night. Someone in the bar moved his car to a safer location. I continued on back to base.

When I reported for duty on my first swing shift with Trick 4, I first was given the riot act by this Master Sergeant who was to be my work area's Senior Printer Systems Supervisor (SPSS). This man was very difficult to get along with, especially if you got on his wrong side. By not initially processing in when I was supposed to, I became number one guy on the top of his shit list. He said if I even farted wrong that he was going to have my ass. I was introduced to my immediate supervisor and activity center controller. His name was Cecil and we had already met. He was the guy I met sitting in his car the night before. Cecil counseled me on what was expected of me as the Activity Center Three controller. I found out in a hurry that Cecil was the God of the Trick 4 printer system operations world. I eventually wanted to be as good as Cecil and from that first night I worked very hard at learning as much as I could about the overall 6921st printer systems mission. I tried to learn his techniques but he wasn't one to take the time to impart all his knowledge to me. He also never gave me a pat on the back or complimented me on a job well done. But, we became friends anyway and I found out that he was a loner when he ran the bars downtown. Periodically I would be running the bars by myself and I would run into him at what I considered an off-the-wall bar that the American's seldom went to. Some of these off-the-wall bars and clubs became some of my favorite haunts. The Amazon and Judy Club were two of the many off-the-beat-and-path places I went to quite often. I also ran into another Trick 4 printer systems operator during my off-the-wall Japanese bar runs. His name was Dan and he almost spoke the Japanese language to perfection. We of course became good friends.

A popular eating and drinking establishment during my first tour at Misawa was located east of the Amazon Club on the same street. The name of this place was the Neutral. After the curfew hour this place became jammed packed. The food was great, especially after a person had quite a few drinks under his or her belt. But I didn't particularly like the Neutral's food when I was sober. About three months after I arrived at Misawa Pat and I were eating at the Neutral after curfew when the town patrol came into the place. Pat and I were both drinking alcoholic beverages and not eating any of Neutrals food. We were apprehended for breaking the curfew regulation. The town patrol took us back to the Air Police station on base and after they got the required information they needed they told us to report to our first sergeant the next morning.

Pat and I both received a letter of reprimand (my second since arriving at Misawa) from the unit orderly room. I was warned that if I continued my trend of getting into trouble while at Misawa that there was a strong possibility of receiving a more severe punishment. We were also told by the first sergeant that we were both being classified as Phase 3 drinkers. As I recall, the first sergeant told us that he had people watching us and that his definition of a Phase 3 drinker was someone who spent more than half or 3/4ths of their paychecks on alcohol. Personally, I never really did believe anything he told us about the Phase 3 classification. I believed and still believe it was the first sergeants attempt to get us to dial our alcohol consumption down. He was right about one thing. I was spending most of my pay at the bars and clubs in downtown Misawa and other cities. There were several personnel that had been informed by the first sergeant that they had been classified as Phase 3 drinkers. I decided to have a Phase 3 patch made for my flight jacket. At the time I thought it was a cool idea.

The Trick 4 Phase 3 Drinker Patch

One on my co-workers by the name of Dan (nicknamed Misfit) had arrived at Misawa in 1966 and was still in Misawa. I loved running the Japanese bars with him because he spoke a little Japanese and of course knew where the hot spots were. He told me that when he started work in 1966 the operational flights worked a 3 Swing, 24 hrs off, 3 Mids, 24 hrs off, 3 Days, 72 hrs off

(3-1-3-1-3-3) shift schedule. When I arrived we were working the 4-1-4-1-4-3 shift schedule. Dan told me about the fire that almost burned down Misawa and the

May1968 earthquake which did some extensive damage to the town and the base. I learned as much as I could from Dan before he was transferred to Darmstadt, Germany in June 1970.

Just up the street from the Amazon Club on the right side were two alleys we called "Sake Alley". All the bars and sake houses in these two alleys were quite small and a very few had inside toilet facilities. If you needed to pee, you stepped outside and use one of the open benjo ditches that ran along side of these places. Mainly the local Japanese populace frequented Sake Alley and only a few from base that I knew drank in these places. I of course was one of the few. On the left side of this same street was a block long two story series of bars. Besides being curious about these Bars and clubs outside the areas that the American servicemen hung out at, I mainly went to these places because of the local curfew. The further I was away from AP Alley I usually had a head start on keeping away from the town patrol. So I learned all the small walking alleys and side streets of Misawa and always tried to keep out of sight of the roving town patrols. We actually weren't bothered by the town patrol if were just walking down the streets and not causing any problems or disturbance. We were allowed to be at local restaurants after curfew to eat meals, but not just consuming alcoholic beverages.

Two Sake Alleys parallel to each other in Misawa

Misawa Covered Alley

Misawa Concrete Alley off "B" Battery Road

All four tricks had off-duty Trick clubs that were all famous in downtown Misawa. Trick-3 had the "Thirsty Thirteen", Trick-1 had the "Rock Club" and Trick-4 sort of had a few different clubs. I don't remember what the name of the Trick-2 club or even if they ever had a club. These clubs changed with time and new personnel. I don't know who the original Trick-3 Thirsty Thirteen people were, but whenever one of its members departed for whatever reason, the empty memberships were filled by a majority vote by the present members of the club. The initiation was held at the Toy's Bar in AP alley and the new member had to shoot-the-pan (a metal wash basin pan full of a conglomeration of different alcoholic beverages selected from the bar's inventory of booze). Pat was the newest member selected to the Thirsty Thirteen and I was there to watch the initiation. All over the walls of the Toy's bar were pictures of previous initiations and in all of these pictures the individuals were spewing forth a stream of barf. Well, Pat accomplished the same feat. He chugged half of this horrible mixture from the pan and then barfed all over the placed. His picture was on one of bar walls the following week. I think most of the Tricks had people shoot the Pan at Toys. This tradition wasn't solely a Trick III Thirsty Thirteen activity. The Trick-1 "Rock Club" had no limit to how many members there could be. I heard that when the rock club members ran the bars in town they better have had their personal rock on their person. If they didn't I understood that they were required to buy at least one round of drinks while on that bar run. I don't remember if Trick-4 had a club with rules or initiations. All trick personnel had trick colored windbreaker jackets with all kinds of patches, including their trick's organization or club patches.

Outside the main gate on the left hand side of the road was a parking lot in front of the Pass and ID building. Also in the parking lot area was a base snack bar. Across from this parking lot and next to the main street was a concrete alley that had two bars next of a public bathhouse. One of these bars was called the Michi Bar. This was a popular first radio hangout. There was an upstairs area in this bar that was primarily used as a card playing room. A mixture of Japanese and GI's would play poker and Japanese rules blackjack. This activity was illegal at that time and the girls downstairs, I think had a warning button located beneath the bar when local police or town patrol entered the bar or was known to be on the way there. If the police were to catch anyone gambling they would confiscate all the money showing on the table. I heard this had happened in other parts of Misawa, but I never personally witnessed it happening at Michi's.

Black Jack Card game at the Michi Bar

There were four bars in town that I used bar tabs at. They were Toys, Trick, Michi and the Jupiter bars. If I were to go through this part of my life again I would never have utilized this idiotic stupid bar bill system. Each payday I would fork over most of my pay to these four places. When I was partaking in most of the Misawa Machi bar runs, not only did I drink too much I was always buying other people drinks and putting it on my bar tab. The bar tabs added up quickly, too quickly.

1969 Toys Bar during the day

1966 Toys Bar during a winter night

1969 Trick Bar during the day

Toy the owner of Toys

To the east of Misawa were the beach areas along the northern Pacific Ocean. Along the beach road going north was the area called Sabishiro and the Ripsaw range. Sabishiro became famous in 1931 when Clyde Pangborn and Hugh Herndon completed the first non-stop Trans-Pacific flight from Japan to the United States. There is a monument near the beach commemorating their feat. Sabishiro was also locally well known for its mental institution.

Pangborn-Herndon monument near Sabishiro

When you went south from Sabishiro you ended up in the city of Hachinohe. Located outside of Hachinohe was a Japanese Self Defense Air Force (JASDAF) base that was also utilized as the local domestic airport during my first and second tours at Misawa. Like

Misawa there was an area of town that had all the bars and clubs and lot of them. A couple of the more known sex orientated attractions was the Manon Theater/DX Club off route 45. Mostly Columbian and Philippine girls from what I saw. Hachinohe was also nationally known for its decorative carved wooden Hachinohe horses. We used these undecorated wooden horses, which people would sign, for sayonara gifts to people leaving Misawa.

The outside of the Manon Theater/DX Club

Pat and I were picked up again for another curfew violation. We gave the town patrol a good run for their money but in the end they got us. Pat had to be cuffed because he began fighting with the town patrol. They locked him up in the drunk-tank and took me back to my dorm. Pat and I both received a Non-Judicial punishment (Article-15) and a fine from the Security

Wing Commander. At work my SPSS was really getting pissed off at me. I was becoming well known for all the wrong reasons. Cecil tried his best to help me out but didn't want to go too far out on the limb to assist me. I was receiving outstanding performance reports from Cecil because I worked real hard and did a great job for him. Most of these great performance reports got downgraded at a higher level. Cecil warned me to watch my back and quite associating with the undesirables of Misawa.

Trying not to get into trouble one day I traveled to Towada City. Towada City was previously known as Rokunohe. I don't know when the town was renamed to Towada City. Most of the locals still referred the town as Rokunohe. Anyway I tried to find some good bars to hang out at. There wasn't too many that I was impressed with. I ended that particular night returning from Towada City at the Misawa train station. Instead of going back to the base, I had lain down onto one of the train station's benches and went to sleep. When I awoke, I found that I had no shoes (Which seemed to happen to me quite often). There was a Japanese man sleeping on a bench next to the one I had slept on and his shoes were sitting next to that bench. I took his shoes and smashed down the heels and used them as sort of a slipper. I caught a taxi back to the base and later wondered what that man did when he realized his shoes were missing. During the winter months my shoes always got soaking wet and sometimes I would take my shoes off and try to dry them off next to the pot belly stoves in the bars. There were a few instances where I would continue my drinking at nearby bars and forget my shoes.

The Tricks had what they called "Roll-Calls" after last mid watches and sometimes after the last day watches. I think the reason they had the Roll Calls after each last mid was so that a person would stay awake as long as they could so that when they did go to sleep, they would wake up the next morning ready for the first day watch. If you didn't stay up (they used the term "Hang") after the last mid a person would normally wake up early in the evening and had a hard time going back to sleep to prepare for the next day watch. The reason for the periodic roll calls after the last day watch was just to celebrate the end of our grueling 14 days of shift work and the beginning of our 72-hour break time.

After one of our last day watches, I was preparing myself for one of our roll calls when one of the guys that lived in the dorm asked me if I wanted a ride down to town. Since it was snowing and the temperature was in the teens, I accepted his ride. Actually there were five of us riding with him. Anyway, after he left the parking area in front of the dorm he picked up a dummy microphone that was tied to the dashboard of the car and talked into the microphone as if it worked. As he was very slowly driving out of the dormitory area he said into the microphone "Fasten your seatbelts gentlemen, we are taxiing to the end of the runway". As we pulled up in front of the orderly room he came to a complete stop. With his foot still on the brake, the car's Hydro-Drive in the drive mode, he started pushing onto the gas pedal. The car started having what sounded like internal hemorrhaging. He then said "Prepare for take-off" and as he let go of his brake we sped off down the hill and ending up at the off-base parking lot. I was surprised that he made it through his tour at Misawa without getting into a serious accident.

That very same night after hitting most of my favorite bars in town, I ended up at Jack's Bar in AP alley. There was a josan in this place that everyone called Shovel Face. Her face looked like it had been smashed with a shovel, but she had a great body. Anyway, I convinced her to let me go home with her that night. I had been drinking what everyone called "Sneaky Pete's" (A Sapporo beer and Akadama red wine mixture) off and on during the night and was really messed up. Shovel Face called for a taxi and took me home with her. A few minutes after I got it on with our sexual activities, I got real sick. Before I could climb off her, I barfed all over her face and the pillow. She shoved me off her and was screaming at me that she was going to kill me. Just as I got me underpants on and grabbed the rest of my cloths and Parka, she entered the bedroom with a butcher knife. I threw a blanket on her and pushed her to the floor and ran out the front door as fast as I could. About two blocks away from her house I stopped, put my Parka on and was going to put my pants on when I noticed her running down the street after me, waving her knife at me and screaming that she was going to kill me. I took off running and didn't stop until I got to the main gate security shack of the base. The Japanese guard and the two AP's that were on patrol and at the gate saw me running towards base wearing only my parka and underwear with shovel face in hot pursuit. There was snow on the ground and the temperature was in the twenties. My feet were wet and cold and I was shivering like hell. The Air police put me into their patrol car and I finished getting the rest of my clothing on. At the same time I watched the Japanese guard try and calm down Shovel Face. Eventually the guard got Shovel Face calmed down and retrieved a taxi, which took Shovel Face back to her house. The Air Police got me into a base taxi that took me back to my dormitory on the hill. I figured that I would be going to see the commander again, but I guess the two AP's (Which I was becoming well acquainted with) did not report the incident to the orderly room. I never returned to Jack's bar the remainder of that tour at Misawa and I never ran into Shovel Face again until six years later. That's another story you will hear later in this book.

I was more or less forced into leaving town quite often due to the fact that I was picked up again by the town patrol for violating the curfew regulation. I was directed to report to the 6921st Security Wing Commander. After reporting to him, he read me my rights. Since I had no leg to stand on and would not have won the battle against this charge, I waived the right to have a lawyer present and then he charged me with another Article-15. He gave me another chance at having a lawyer and I again waived that choice. He then threw the book at me. My punishment was a fine and a warning that I would be losing my E-4 Senior Airman rank if I was to continue my off-duty misdeeds. My Non-Judicial punishments were beginning to add up.

One of the downsides of my continuing problems with the rules and regulations at that time was that my Air Force career was in dire straits. The upside (If you can call it that) was that I was spending a lot of time out of Misawa. This required me to use what little conversational Japanese my brain was accumulating and I always carried my pocket English – Japanese Dictionary. I was actually slowly learning some of the language, even if it was mostly just bar talk. One of my main problems with all the trouble I was getting into was due to the people I associated with during my off-duty hours. I hung out with some of the hardest hardcore bar runners in Misawa which were people from three of the four Tricks and a few from other main base organizations. These people always seemed to be in town whenever I was. The Japanese phrase for this type of person was Machi Nezumi or Tanuki (Town Rat). Some of the Japanese stores sold stuffed statues of these Machi Nezumi's. The stuffed nezumi held in one hand a bar bill or ledger and in the other hand, the Nezumi held a bottle of sake.

I spent my first spring in Misawa getting out of Misawa on most of my 72-hour breaks. I would either stay in another town over my breaks or just leave Misawa around 1000 or 1100 each night and take a bus or train to the nearby cities of Hachinohe, Aomori or Towada City to do my bar hoping without worry of being picked up by the town patrol. When I wanted to get off base and out of town for an entire break or on leaves, I either went to Hirosaki, Aomori-Ken prefecture or Hakodate, Oshima-Ken prefecture. Hirosaki is nestled amongst the mountains that were located southwest of Aomori city. Hakodate is one of the most southern port cities on the Island of Hokkaido.

I was told that if I wanted to have a great time that I should go to the Cherry Blossom Festival at Hirosaki. My friend Dan told me about this place he always stayed at by the name of Ishiba Ryokan (Japanese style hotel). So I went to Hirosaki on one of my breaks that coincided with the Cherry Blossom Festival at Hirosaki. I stayed at the Ishiba Ryokan. The Ryokan was about two blocks from the Hirosaki Park and Hirosaki Castle.

Hirosaki-Shi Ishiba Ryokan

While walking around the city I noticed that all the manhole covers located on the Hirosaki streets had what looked like a Nazi Swastika symbol on them. I misinterpreted this symbol. This symbol had been around long before the Nazi Party thought of their swastika symbol. I also think that the symbol was in reverse of that of the Nazi Swastika. When I asked one of the bartenders at one of bars about what the symbol stood for he told me that the symbol was embedded in the Hinduism and Buddhism religions. It meant something like luck or well-being. At Hirosaki Park there is a beautiful panoramic view of a snow covered Mt Iwaki. This dormant volcano looked like it was same shape as Mt Fuji. Further south and closer to Hirosaki was Mt Ajara where the Owani Onsen ski resort is located. At Hirosaki Park I got into a conversation with a couple of college students and ended up sitting on one of the park's grass areas amongst about 15 or 16 Japanese students and drinking cold and hot sake with them. I later ended up running the bars and clubs with the three of these students. This was the beginning in my education of knowing where to go and not to go in Hirosaki. Of course just about any town in Japan would have been a better place to run the bars than Misawa at that time.

Crooked Cross Symbol on a Manhole cover

Hirosaki Castle built in 1611

Hirosaki Park Pagoda

Mount Iwaki

Mount Iwaki near Hirosaki

During the summer months Misawa city celebrated several festivals (Matsuri). They were the Tanabata

Matsuri, Bon Odori Matsuri held in July and the San Sha Tai Sai Matsuri and the Nebuta Matsuri held in August. The largest and more famous Nebuta Matsuri's were held in Aomori and Hirosaki. I loved the smell and taste of the Japanese foods that some of the vendors cooked up during all of these festivals. During the Misawa City festivals the smell of barbecued food drifted onto the base and a person couldn't help wanting to go downtown and try out some of the food they were serving. During my first Tanabata Matsuri I was walking all over town trying out the vender's food items and watching the festivities. Some of the vendors at both festivals sold baby chickens, ducklings and gold fish in plastic bags that were filled with water. Throughout my first Tanabata Matsuri I would periodically go to the Michi Bar to rest and have a few drinks (a pit stop). During one of my late afternoon pit stops at the Michi Bar, there was a guy sitting at the bar with his head resting on his arms. I assumed he was either asleep or passed out. There was a little duckling walking back and forth on top of the bar. The duckling was making quite a racket with all its quacking. The duckling waddled back and forth in front of this guy that was either sleeping or passed out. No one paid much attention to or was bothered by the duckling. At least that's what I thought. Suddenly this guy that was supposedly sleeping at the bar rose to his feet and as the duckling came waddling passed him, the guy screamed "shut the fuck up" and smashed the duckling with his fist and of course instantly killing the duckling.

He threw the dead duckling onto the bar floor and went back to his sleeping position at the bar. When he smashed the duck the bar went deathly quiet and then everyone broke out into a roaring laughter after witnessing the smashing of the poor little duckling. About an hour later several people from Trick I were in the Michi bar and most of them had been drinking most of the day. One of the Trick-I guys dared this guy called Tex to eat some live goldfish that someone had brought into the bar. Tex said that someone would have to make it worth his attempt. Several people in the bar including myself all chipped in some Japanese Yen & MPC, which added up to over to a small bundle of cash. But before Tex could have the money we told him that he had to eat all the goldfish followed by eating a live baby chicken. Tex accepted our terms and first ate all the goldfish. He then took a deep breath and stuck the baby chicken into his mouth headfirst. The baby chicken's legs were moving all over the place as Tex starting crunching it with his teeth. As Tex was crunching away he was pushing the little chicken with his fingers to get it forced into his mouth. After several minutes Tex had completely devoured the little chicken. He wiped the blood and feathers away from his face and grabbed a beer and his prize money. No one could believe his or her eyes; Tex actually ate the baby chicken. Hours later Tex was having very bad stomach pains and was taken to the base emergency room. He was kept overnight and I heard that besides Tex doing a lot of vomiting, he also had his stomach pumped. At any rate he was one sick puppy.

On another one of my 72-hour breaks during the summer months, I returned to Hirosaki and stayed at a same Ryokan I had previously stayed at the last time I was in Hirosaki. On this visit I decided to venture out to the Owani Onsen Ski Resort area and take the chair lift up the mountain so I could take some pictures of the panoramic view of the Hirosaki & Owani areas. On the chair lift ride up the mountain there was a Shinto shrine located amongst some gnarly trees about halfway up the mountain. The view from the top of the mountain was breathtaking.

Owani Onsen Ski Resort chair lifts during the summer months

While taking my photographs, I noticed some Japanese hikers descending down and away from the chair lift on a hiking trail. So I decided to explore this trail to see where it went. About 45 minutes later I met the same Japanese hikers that I had seen earlier returning back up the trail. Looking down the mountain, the trail looked like it ended up near a river. I think the name of the river is Hira, but I'm not sure. I had trekked so far down the mountain trail that I didn't want to attempt climbing back up to the chair lift area atop of this mountain. By the time I reached a paved road it was getting dark. After walking along the road I finally arrived at the small town of Owani that was on the outskirts of Hirosaki. I noticed there were a few snack and bar establishments. I entered one of the bars and I was definitely out of place there. More of an oddity I think. Anyway, I bought everyone that entered the place a few drinks and of course they reciprocated. Everyone I attempted to talk to tried teaching me new Japanese words and phrases. The mama-san was kind enough to get me something to eat and after my brain was overloaded with the new Japanese phrases, wore out from the long walk in the sun and numb from too many drinks, I passed out at the bar counter. I awoke the next morning in the back room of the bar. The mama-san and whoever else was at the bar when they closed up must have carried me to the back room and covered me with a blanket. The mama-san's home was behind the bar and when I was getting ready to leave, she came to the bar with some scrambled eggs and rice for me to eat. After I ate her welcomed breakfast, I asked her if she would call me a taxi and thanked her for her hospitality. After arriving back at the ryokan, I took a long hot bath and slept the rest of the day. After another night out on the town in the bar areas of Hirosaki, I reluctantly went back to Misawa and another 14-day cycle of work.

I was an avid skier during my high school years and on my first Air Force assignment in Germany. After arriving in the Far East, skiing was an afterthought. If I was able to go back in time I would have taken advantage of the northern Honshu ski resorts available to me like Moya Hills Ski Resort about 8 mile out of Aomori, Owani Onsen Ski Resort outside of Hirosaki and the Hakkoda Ski Resort about an hour's drive from Aomori. This didn't happen of course and like other overseas assignments I had to accept that I couldn't do and see everything.

After attending and hanging one of our Trick's last mid roll calls, I went to Aomori to spend the afternoon and then came back to Misawa. I continued to run the bars and ended up staying with one of the josans that worked in AP alley. I didn't wake up until my first day watch was half over. I called my supervisor Cecil and told him that I had overslept. Since the shift was almost over, I was told to report to work the next day. After arriving for duty the next day I was escorted over to the orderly room with my immediate supervisor and the SPSS. After the two supervisors came out of the unit commander's office I was instructed to report to the unit commander. I was given my rights and after going through the usual procedures I was given another Article 15, a monitory fine and on top of all that I was restricted to the base for 30 days.

Two days later after the last day watch I decided to ignore the restriction order and I got a ride off base and went to one of my favorite haunts away from the bars near the base. Early that same evening I was turning the corner from a side alley onto the main street of town when I ran into my SPSS. He asked me why I was downtown and not on base. I told him that I was just coming down to get something to eat at one of the local restaurants. He then told me that I was breaking the commander's restriction order and that it was his duty as a responsible NCO to report me to the Air Police and the unit commander. I couldn't understand his reasoning of course and called him a flaming asshole and continued onto AP alley to finish my bar running.

On the last day of that 72-hour break I received a message from the unit's orderly room to report to the unit commander prior to my first swing shift. The usual crowd was there and this time my trick/flight commander was also present. I received another Article 15, loss of my E-4 rank and this time was also ordered into correctional custody at the Air Police facility on main base. I really wasn't surprised of being demoted, but wasn't expecting to be put into the correctional facility on main base. I also received a letter stating that I was being placed onto the Airman Control Roster for a period of 90 days. Basically I could not mess up at all during this period and I had to correct all my misguided behavior patterns and satisfactorily meet with the current Air Force standards. I was to receive a special performance report at the end of this 90-day period.

During correctional custody I spent every night in a jail cell and during the day I reported to my unit's first sergeant. He would assign each weekday's duties to me. These duties were usually yard work, painting, picking up litter, etc., around the hill area of the base. On the weekends the correctional custody members had jail cell area and uniform inspections. Also on weekends when we went to eat our meals, two air policemen always escorted us to and from the chow hall. On Saturdays we also washed vehicles at the base transportation depot. On Sundays, we chased and captured stray dogs. You could get out of the stray dog patrol duty if you attended the base church services. I decided on the church services instead of chasing dogs the last two Sundays of my detention. I had a cellmate that was in correctional custody for physically attacking some NCO or his commander. I don't know the whole story. He never told me what happened. I was told by a couple of the Air Policemen that he had spent a tour in South Vietnam and was transferred to Misawa. When processing into his main base orderly room he was told by an orderly room NCO or commander (don't know which) to get his hair and handlebar mustache cut within Air Force 35-10 regulations. That is when this guy blew up and attacked the NCO or commander. He was kicked out of the Air Force six months later as a slick sleeve airman.

When I was on my last week in correctional custody, my friend Pat unexpectedly visited me. Since I wasn't allowed visitors, he came to my opened screened in cell window. He was drunk and wasn't making too much sense. He said he had plans on breaking me out of jail so we could run the bars downtown. I told Pat to get the hell away from the window and leave me alone. I told him that if he didn't leave he was going to get me into a lot more trouble. The funny thing about this episode was that the Air Police saw Pat walk up to the building and then watched and listened to the both of us. They told me later that they were wondering what Pat would actually attempt to do. Pat finally got tired of arguing with me and departed. The Air Police shift supervisor told me that I didn't need friend like Pat. The day of my release the Air Police commander told me that there were several people waiting for me outside the Air Police facility. These friends of mine had planned a getting-out party for me at the Toy's bar in AP Alley. He advised me that I had better take all my future actions into serious consideration and be on the straight and narrow from here on out or I would more than likely be unfavorably discharged from the Air Force.

At my party one of my gifts was a new patch for my trick jacket. The words **Article 15 Club President** with roman numerals depicting Article 15's was inscribed onto this patch. I received four of these Article 15's during my first year at Misawa. I had the patch sewed onto my trick jacket and everyone thought I was one cool dude for accomplishing this feat. I used this patch to remind me of how stupid I was to have received them. Either the correctional custody punishment or my own realization of how I probably had screwed myself out of making the Air Force a career finally knocked some sense into me. I cut my drinking time and bar running to after the last mid shifts, after the last day watches and break time and spent my energies at learning all I could at work. My good behavior was rewarded with me being taken off the Airman Control

Roster after receiving an outstanding rating on my 90 day special performance report.

Article 15 Patch that was sewn onto my flight Jacket

During the summer we sometimes went to the beach near Sabishiro and partied. During one such party I was with a couple of guys from Trick-II. Rowdy from Idaho (he looked like Rowdy Yates in the show Rawhide), Walt from Minnesota and I did some body surfing, beer drinking and beach combing. I actually found a couple of Japanese glass floats, which I have to this day. We came back from the beach and went to Toy's in AP alley and continued our drinking. We were wearing cutoff jeans and had sand in our hair and on our bodies. Walt was wearing a Japanese military helmet liner that he had found at the beach and a thick rope around his neck. It became late afternoon and Walt and Rowdy wanted to go back to their dorm on the hill. I was not as drunk as they were and told them I would go back with them on the base bus to the hill and their dorm. Believe it or not I got no argument from them. On the way to the hill, they passed out. I was able to get Rowdy awake and he sort of helped me carry Walt off the bus and up the outside stairs to their dorm. When we got to the upstairs door, Rowdy let go of Walt and put his fist through the door window and cut himself. I got Walt inside the dorm and down onto the hallway floor and then got Rowdy into the bathroom and told him that he should go to the clinic on main base. Rowdy was having none of that and he said that the cut wasn't that bad. Rowdy later went to the clinic and received several stitches for his wounds. Anyway, I got Rowdy to his room and put some makeshift bandages on his cut hand and told him that if he wasn't going to the clinic that he needed to go to bed. Then I went out and with help from a couple of other people got Walt into his room. While we were in Walt's room Rowdy came stumbling into the room with the hallway phone in his hand. He said that Walt had a phone call and started laughing and fell to the floor. At that time I decided to leave my two friends from Trick-II and go back to my dorm and hoped my name wasn't given to the commander. Luckily, my name wasn't brought to our commander's attention. Walt and Rowdy received Article-15's and had to pay for the damages incurred in their dorm.

Of all the after the last mid-shift roll calls in AP Alley, I only have two photos that I am in. This photo was of a roll call I attended at the Toys Bar in 1970.

Roll Call gathering outside the Toys Bar

There were several 292X1's (later changed to 207X1's – we called them Ditty-Boppers) that were transferred to flying status and sent for a tour of duty in South Vietnam. Some of these guys deployed in South Vietnam decided to take their R&R at Misawa, Japan. We set up a party for them at Toys during the daytime on one of our breaks. During our party one of the guys noticed an American flag hanging from the balcony outside of the Owl coffeehouse. On the flag was painted a black Nazi Swastika. The Owl coffeehouse was where the anti-war and anti-American involvement in South Vietnam people hung out (Japanese & American alike). Someone from the party at Toys spotted the flag called everyone out to look at this disgrace. About 12 guys decided to go upstairs into the place and get the American flag taken down. The coffeehouse was on the second floor of the building. As a bunch of us were standing out in the alley, a chair came through the upstairs window and landed in the alley below. There was a bunch of yelling and screaming and the sound of things being broken within the place. While we were standing there a Japanese police car drove up with his red lights blinking. I knew one of the policemen. I ran into him from time to time when I was running the bars in town. Anyway, he asked me what the problem was and we all pointed up at the American flag. The two policemen stood and watched what was going on for a few minutes and then they smiled at us and told us to try and stop our guys from doing any more damage and then departed. As soon as the Japanese police left, one of our guys came out onto the balcony and retrieved the defiled American flag. After the ruckus we went back to our party at Toys. I don't know if owner of the owl put in a complaint or request for payment on damages or not. Local base police asked a few questions and I never heard any more about it after that.

There were two guys that I sometimes ran the bars with in Misawa that were on my trick. Phil (A Ditty-Bop) and a guy we called Pudgy (an Analyst). One break after we had been running the bars for several hours, Phil and Pudgy decided that instead of alluding the town patrols they were going out of town via a train to continue their bar running. I had far too much to drink and I kept on falling asleep wherever we went in the latter stages of our bar run. Anyway, we ended up down at Furamaki and the Misawa Train Yard. Pudgy and Phil decided that they were not going to pay for the train ride and somehow got me onto a ledge between two train cars and then they went and climbed onto the front engine car and I guess tried to get the engine to go. I don't know how Phil and pudgy ended up getting access to the trains engine but they did it. Don't ask me what or how it happened, but somehow I had climbed down off the train and ended up sleeping in between two building just off the train yard at Misawa. When I awoke and got back to my dorm on the hill, I was unaware of what had happened to Phil and Pudgy. The next day I found out that they were both arrested by the Japanese police for trying to steal that freight train and turned over to the base authorities. Someone must have been looking after me and made me crawl off that train or I would have been in a heap of shit. Besides ending up having to personally apologize to the Misawa train office, Phil & Pudgy also had to pay monitory fines to the Japanese train office and to top that off they were both given article 15's by our unit commander. This train episode got blown all out of proportion through my remaining years in the Air Force. Every time I told the train story to someone I blew it out of proportion and I always involved myself in the story as if I was one of the three that were involved when it was only Phil and Pudgy that were arrested and punished.

There were a few bars that were open day and night in AP alley. I can't remember the name of this one bar that stayed open day and night, but this place was later called the Boom Boom Bar.

Anyway, whenever I was down in AP alley during the daytime I would always go there. It seemed like every time I went to this bar, I would find this guy sitting at the far end of the bar. He always seemed to have several books laid in front of him and he never seemed to acknowledge that I was also in the bar. Anyway to get on with this story, I was running the bars one evening and was drinking "Sneaky Pete's". Just before midnight I staggered into the Naples restaurant in AP alley, sat on one of the revolving stools at the counter, and ordered some spaghetti. Everything that happened at Naples was related to me the next day. While waiting for my meal I turned and faced this guy sitting at one of the small tables and yelled at him to get the fuck out of Naples before I beat the shit out of him. He ignored me and I guess I yelled at him a couple more times and then shut up when my spaghetti was brought to me. I was about to eat my spaghetti when I passed out headfirst into the plate of spaghetti that was sitting in front of me. The guy I was yelling at saw what had happened of course. He came to the counter and lifted my head out of the plate of spaghetti, moved the plate and then dropped my head onto the bar counter. When I woke up the next day I had a sore nose and a throbbing headache. Except for the sore nose, I basically thought it was a horrible hangover from the night before.

A day later I went into the bar that I was always seeing that guy with all his books. After I had ordered my drink the guy surprised me with an unexpected statement. He said that from that point on, if I was to ever speak to him the way I had in the Naples restaurant that he would kick the shit out of me. I of course didn't know what the hell he was talking about. So I approached him and asked him a lot of questions. I was of course really embarrassed about what I had done and apologized all over the place to him. I bought him a few drinks and found out his name was Andy. I also found out that he was on his third tour at Misawa and that he presently held a high degree black belt in Korean style Karate. I eventually became a good friend of Andy's and I always liked running the bars with him. Andy spoke fluent conversational Japanese and was going to school on base to learn how to read and write the Japanese language.

During the sixties there were three bars in AP alley that had a few good looking hammers, the New Tokyo, Top Hat and Metro bars. The main problem with going to these bars was that the hammers continually bothered us about buying them ladies drinks. Whenever we had bar runs, we would always visit these three places. We sometimes would buy a few of the better looking hammers their ladies drinks and then made bets amongst ourselves about the hammers panties. Was she wearing panties? If she was wearing panties what color were they? As long as we continued to supply the hammers their ladies drinks the hammers usually obliged us by showing off what they were or were not wearing and then we settled our bets and went on our merry way to another bar.

On one of our trick roll-call runs we pre-planned playing a joke on the hammers in the New Tokyo bar. I had seen some GI's in the Philippines play the "can of vegetable soup trick". So on one of our bar-hopping runs I brought a can of vegetable soup with me. I went into the (1) benjo and opened the can of soup and then went back to the bar. When none of the hammers were in my area of the bar, I poured the soup on the bar and faked the sound of puking. All the hammers thought I had barfed on the bar. Anyway, as soon as I faked the puking, everyone around me started grabbing parts of the soup and eating the pieces they had picked up. Our rude display really grossed out the mama-san and the hammers and we enjoyed every minute of that particular joke we played on them.

In the fall of 1969 our trick had a trip over one of our breaks to the city of Hakodate on the northern island of Hokkaido. We took the train to Aomori and then we traveled by ship to Hakodate. Hakodate lies at the neck of the Hakodate peninsula, with Mt Hakodate rising up at its tip. After checking into one of the western style hotels, we were free to do what we wanted until the next day. So I went to find the bar and club area which was located near the harbor and then decided to find out how to get up to the top of Mount Hakodate. I was given directions by one of the information booths at the train station that it was about 3 Kilometers in distance from the train station and the best way for me to get to the tramway was by streetcar. After arriving at the tramway station, I took the 5-10 minute tramway to the top of Mt Hakodate and the view of the Tsugaru Straits, Hakodate Bay, port and the city was impressive to say the least. There was a portrait monument dedicated to an Englishman named Thomas Wright Blakiston, which seemed kind of strange since we were in Japan. I think he was a famous naturalist. Anyway after taking several photographs the sun started setting in the west and the lights of the city started coming on, I waited to until it got dark and took some night pictures of Hakodate. The darker it got the prettier the view of the city became.

(1)Benjo – *Outside drainage ditch or the Men's and Women's toilet room*.

155

Hakodate City from Mount Hakodate

Thomas Blakiston monument on Mount Hakodate

Three of us explored the bars and clubs that night and got back to our hotel about two in the morning. The next day a bus took all of us to this old western style fort called Goryokaku. This old fortification was in the shape of a star. There is now a nearby tower to get an overhead angle of the entire star configured fortification. From the star fort we took the bus again and arrived at this trappistine convent. These trappist monks adhere to a vow of absolute silence. Unless I was physically incapable of talking, I myself could not imagine not being able to talk. Maybe that's why there weren't too many trappistine monks there. The trappistine monks engaged in caring for stock animals and worked an active dairy farm. They produced local butter and candy to the Japanese market.

I spent that last night in Hakodate again exploring the bar district and applying what little Japanese I knew on the bar hammers. I met this one hammer that had natural red hair and found out that she was a half-breed. Her father was a Russian fisherman and her mother was Japanese. She gave me her address and phone number and told me that the next time I was in Hakodate that she would like for us to get together. Like a fool, I lost her address and phone number and the next time I went to Hakodate, she no longer worked at the bar that I met her at.

The mama-san named Kay (I think the name was actually Keiko) that ran the Jupiter bar in AP alley was a good-looking hammer that I continually tried to get her into bed with me. All I ever end up accomplishing was going to lunch or dinner with her and I never got any further than that. I would be in the Jupiter begging her to go to bed with me and was always telling her how horny I was and desperately needed a piece of ass. She just laughed at me and said maybe someday that she could set me up with someone. This scenario went on for months until one evening she said that she had someone lined up for me. She said that the girl was from Sendai and that she would be at the Jupiter Bar at about 7 PM the next night. Kay asked if I wanted to go with this girl to one of the local hotels. I agreed to meet this girl the next night.

When I was introduced to her the next night, I could not believe my eyes. She was good looking and looked to be in her mid 20's. We went out to eat and then she called a taxi and we went to this hotel near the train station. In our room she wasted no time in taking all her clothes off and lying onto the bed. The lovemaking was great and of course I was satisfied. But she obviously wasn't ready to quit. She wanted to make love one more time. It took me a while with some foreplay but I was able to make love to her one more time. After that second episode she said that she needed to get back to the Jupiter Bar and talk with Kay. I tried to give her 5,000 Yen and added that I was willing to pay for the hotel. She declined the 5,000 yen and said the bill was already paid for in advance. We both took a shower and got dressed and went back to the Jupiter bar. She talked with Kay for about 15 minutes and then thanked me for the wonderful evening and then said goodbye. I asked Kay if there was any way that I could get together with this hammer again sometime soon. Kay said that I would probably never be able to be with her again and would never tell me why. A couple of months later as I entered the Jupiter bar I was astonished to see this gorgeous hammer sitting with this Japanese guy in one of the back corner seats. She looked away from me when I looked at her and I sat at the bar and started asking questions. Kay asked me to come outside the bar into the alley with her and I did so. Kay said that this josan was married to the guy she was with and would I please try to act like I didn't know her. To this day I don't understand why she had that one night stand with me. My hands were shaking so badly; I could hardly hold the drink that I had carried out into the alley with me. I was sweating and really embarrassed about the whole situation. And then Kay handed me this fancy envelope with a ribbon on it. Inside the envelope was some Japanese Yen. I said, "What's this for". Kay said it was a gift from the hammer. I tried giving the money and envelope back to Kay, but she wouldn't take it and she told me that this josan would be shammed if she was to take the money back. Was I paid for this sexual encounter? I felt like I was sort of used, but didn't regret that it happened.

On another one of my 72 hour breaks I was asked by one of the married co-workers if I wanted to go with him and his wife to Lake Towada. Since I had never been there, I thanked him for asking me and I fell in love with the National Park that Towada Lake was located in. On the way to the lake we drove along the beautiful Oirase River. We stopped at the Oirase Gorge Water Falls and took some pictures. We continued on to the lake and spent the day sightseeing and taking more pictures.

Water falls on the way to Lake Towada

Towada Resort area at Lake Towada

After my tour was half over at Misawa, I had to fill out paperwork for requesting my next duty assignment (We called it a Dream Sheet). I put down the Philippines, South Korea and Thailand for my overseas assignments and Only Washington State on my stateside assignment. Four months prior to my departure date I was called into the orderly room commander's office. He informed me that because of all the trouble I had been into while stationed at Misawa that he was requesting two things from higher headquarters. One – I was to be sent back stateside and not to a follow-up overseas assignment and Two – He was notifying higher headquarters that he was requesting that I not be allowed to re-enlist again in the Air Force. He stated that he thought part of my problems stemmed from being overseas and away from home. My thoughts on this were "what a bunch of horse shit". Two weeks later I was notified by base personnel that I was being sent to the 6993rd Security Squadron at Kelly AFB, San Antonio, Texas. I did not want to go to San Antonio, Texas and believe it or not, I did not want to leave Misawa. I was becoming very comfortable with my life style in Misawa and was actually becoming respected and appreciated for my on-going efforts at work.

I decided that before I left Misawa that I was going to do some partying at Songtan, Korea and visit some friends at the 6903rd Security Group located at Osan AB, South Korea. I took 12 days leave and caught a hop from Misawa to Osan Air Base. I had heard a lot of wild things about the nightlife outside Osan Air Base in Songtan City and wanted to check it out for myself. My old friend Pat also took leave and went along with me.

He had been there on leave once before since our arrival at Misawa. We couldn't get into billeting at Osan Air Base, so had to stay in a hotel just outside the main gate on Aragon Street. I was told that everyone called this street "Rock & Roll Alley". What a bunch of wild establishments. Every establishment had a bar load of hammers and the music was loud. This Sin City of the North brought memories flooding back to me about the good old days in the Philippines. Some of the bars in Rock & Roll Alley were the Scorpion, Happy Horse, Easy Rider, Gold Star, Iron Horse, Heavy Metal, Skinny Mom's, Playboy and on the Main Drag of Songtan city we hung out at the Golden Gate, Merk and the Mob.

My immediate supervisor (Cecil) relieved me from duty two weeks prior to my departure from Misawa. There were several days during that two-week period that I don't remember a damn thing. I was partying every night. The Mama-sans at the Toys & Michi Bars gave me a great going away gift by not requiring me to pay off my bar bills. I know that between the two bars

I owed over two hundred dollars. I also received a wooden Hachinohe horse that co-workers at work and some of the hammers downtown signed. Just one of many sayonara gifts.

Signed Hachinohe Horse

With sadness I left Misawa Air Base and swore to myself that I was going to fight what the 6921st orderly room commander had initiated on me. I wanted to stay in the Air Force.

Chapter 6: 6993 SECURITY SQUADRON,
KELLY AFB
SAN ANTONIO, TEXAS
1971 - 1972

While I was processing into Kelly AFB, I informed the personnel department that I wanted to be allowed to re-enlist for another four years when my present enlistment ended. I told them of the situation that I was in and when it had been initiated in Japan. They told me what recourse I had and I then initiated the proper paperwork to my current commander and whatever decision he made on this re-enlistment request would be final. He was authorized to override my Misawa commander's decision if I proved to him that I would be of value to the command and the Air Force.

The only socializing I did during the first three months was at a bar that was just outside the Kelly AFB Annex gate. I didn't have a car and I did not feel comfortable at that time going anywhere on a bus or with anybody in the San Antonio area. I had to ride a base bus that took me out to the Medina 6993rd Security Squadron operational area when I was on duty. They called our operational area the Medina Annex. I think the annex was actually part of the Lackland AFB Training Center.

My new duties at the 6993rd were pretty boring compared to my duties at previous overseas assignments. But, I had told myself that I was going to prove to my new supervisors and commander that I was worth keeping in the Air Force. In the first three months I volunteered for just about every duty that was available to me at work. I got along with both the Air Force and Army supervisors and was given several critical responsibilities. I even received a letter a commendation for an outstanding duty accomplishment.

I was eventually called into my squadron commander's office for a discussion about my request for re-enlistment. My Flight commander and supervisors were also present. Our unit commander started the meeting off by congratulating me for regaining my Senior Airman stripes (E-4) back and handed me my promotion orders. After listening to my flight commander and supervisor's inputs the unit commander made the decision to approve my re-enlistment action. I immediately went to the personnel office and put in for a transfer for the Philippines, Thailand, Korea or Japan. I also requested for an early release from my current assignment in San Antonio.

At work I had made several friends. Jim and this other guy named Ed were always asking me to go with them when they socialized off-duty at different places in San Antonio. Another guy name Phil worked in the tape library at work. Phil and I became very good friends during my future assignments at Misawa, Japan. Since the pressure was off me because my re-enlistment problems being resolved, I gave in to Jim and Ed's persistent requests to go with them on their excursions to different nightclubs and bars. On one evening they dropped me off at this place just off of Highway 90 near Lackland AFB. They said they would be back for me in about two hours. This joint had girls dancing in front of mirrors and there were numerous guys wearing shit-kicker boots and cowboy hats. When Jim & Ed arrived to pick me up, I made a stupid comment to them about all the assholes in the place dressed up as cowboys (Too many drinks were affecting me). I was overheard making this statement by two of these so-called cowboys and shit hit the fan. Jim & Ed got me out of the place and talked them out of starting anything with me. Jim & Ed were kind of pissed off at me and told me that the next time I said something like that in any of the places we went to that I would have to resolve any problem I got into all by myself.

Some of the places we hung out at with some consistency were the Town Pump off I-35 on St Mary's street, the Crystal Pistol off San Pedro, The Green Lantern along with several other places on Austin Highway. Sometimes we went to the River Walk area establishments, but their drinks were too expensive for us. We only went to the River Walk area on special occasions.

Mostly members of the Army from Fort Sam Houston hung out at the Town Pump. So we Air Force zoomies were kind of outnumbered. One evening we were at the Town Pump and I noticed this young woman smoking a cigar at one of the tables near the dance floor. She seemed to be mingling and dancing with a lot of the guys that were in the bar. She was constantly talking and laughing with everyone she came in contact with. Ed told me her name was Maria and that he would introduce me to her if I wished. I considered his request over a few drinks and then I finally gave in to her charms and asked Ed to introduce us. I found out that she worked at the Southwest Bell Telephone Company and was sharing an apartment with two other girls. I dated Maria for several months, going to Nuevo Laredo, Mexico, Victoria, Texas, Canyon Lake and several local areas outside of San Antonio.

Jim & Louisa in Nuevo Laredo

BBQ at Canyon Lake

I took 30 days leave and Maria & I flew to Washington State. Maria got acquainted with my folks and I showed her my old stomping grounds. My dad gave me an old black Karmann Ghia Volkswagen and we drove Back to San Antonio, stopping to visit relatives and friends in Medford Oregon, Los Angeles California and Phoenix, Arizona. The forth gear gave out on us after we left Phoenix. It would only stay in gear after I put it into 4th gear and the gearshift was secured with rope and the other end of the rope tied to one the car seat struts. We did ok with this quick fix on the open highway, but when going through populated areas it was up to third gear only. After we made it back to San Antonio I had the transmission fixed, but the Volkswagen was on its last legs and I was going to need another car sometime soon.

Two other guys and I were notified that we were selected to go on Sea Duty onboard the USNS Vandenberg. Yea, some of us upper 2 percent Air Force members also spent their time doing their duties at sea. We reported to Pearl Harbor in Honolulu, Hawaii. There was no billeting available so we were checked into a hotel just off the Waikiki Beach area. We spent a week attending briefings during the afternoon hours and the rest of the time each day visiting several of the many beaches on Oahu Island and hanging out at the bars and clubs near our hotel.

USNS Vandenberg

At Adak Island with USNS Vandenberg behind me

While we were on this TDY we were authorized to wear civilian clothing and were not required to shave or get our hair cut. After the USNS Vandenberg arrived at our assigned destination, we were met by Soviet fishing trawlers and a few Soviet naval vessels. There were always a few of these ships near us during our entire stay. On one clear day one these ships had all their onboard women line up on the deck and take off their top attire revealing their breasts to us. Then one of the soviet crewmen fondled some of these women and we responded to them by giving them the finger. After spending three months of duty in the north pacific we returned to the states. We traveled up the Columbia River to Portland, Oregon. My family lived near Seattle, Washington, so I volunteered to courier the classified materials to McChord AFB and then take a few days leave to visit my folks. Our commander rented a station wagon and said he and one other guy would be riding with me to McChord AFB. Our commander was going to be taking a military aircraft back to the east coast and I was to take the other guy to SeaTac Airport after we completed the offload of the classified materials. We loaded up the classified materials and drove to McChord AFB. After getting directions from the Security Policeman at the main gate we proceeded first to the MAC Terminal to drop off our commander. He was going to arrange his flight out of McChord and then meet us later at the vault building. We then proceeded to the classified vault building. Since it was after duty hours when we arrived we had to call an off-duty number to have someone come and take custody of our materials. A shaved headed MSgt arrived 30 minutes later and found us sitting on the steps of the building.

We gave him our paperwork and identification cards. While he was scrutinizing the paperwork he kept checking us out and finally made the statement "You guys can't really be in the Air Force". We told him that we were authorized not to shave get our hair cut during our TDY and were allowed to wear civilian clothes on this particular mission. I don't think he believed us of course and he asked who was in charge, who was our commander. Since our paperwork was in order this MSgt went ahead and took the materials into the vault area of the building, but he still wanted to know who our commander was. Just as we were bringing in the last of our materials, our commander arrived in a base taxi. Even after our commander showed his Air Force credentials to this Master Sergeant he was still skeptical. I guess this Master Sergeant couldn't believe that an Air Force Colonel would grow a beard.

A few months later I asked Maria if she would marry me and she accepted. We were married on 18 December 1971. A few months later I received my new assignment. The Air Force was sending me back to Misawa AB, Japan on an accompanied tour status for three years. This new assignment didn't go over to good with Maria. I think she had second thoughts about going with me to Japan. Included in this reassignment was that I had to attend a five week analysis course at the National Security Agency (NSA) located at Ft Meade, Maryland. While attending the Analysis course I contacted my friend Bob who lived in Maryland. I was stationed with Bob at Clark AB in the Philippines. He only served four years in the Air Force. His first assignment was at Karamursel, Turkey. During my weekends off Bob would pick me up at the barracks and we would hit some of the local bars and clubs. One weekend he drove me to Cumberland, Maryland and he introduced me to his family and again hit the clubs in the Cumberland vicinity.

After attending the analysis course at NSA we decided to buy a new 1972 Karmann Ghia Volkswagen and I wanted it shipped over to Misawa Japan. I was informed by the transportation/shipping office at Kelly AFB that I would be able to have the car shipped from Seattle, Washington. When the time came to leave San Antonio, Maria reluctantly quit her great job at Southwest Bell and we both said our fair-wells to her family and friends. I took leave and we drove to Washington State to visit my family.

1972 Karmann Gia

On our way to Washington

After about a week at home, I took the car ferry over to Seattle and drove to the pier where I was to have my car shipped. The guard at the gate looked at my paperwork, scratched his head and told me that probably the last time cars were shipped from that pier was during the Korean War. They quit shipping cars at that pier after the Korean conflict. I went back to Bremerton and the next day went to the transportation office at the Puget Sound Naval Shipyard (PSNS) and pleaded with them to help me out with my problem. They said that there should be no problem because one of the Navy's aircraft carriers that was at PSNS was transferring to southern Japan and the crew's private owned vehicles (POV's) would be taken to Japan on that aircraft carrier. From southern Japan they would arrange transportation of my POV to Hachinohe via a

Naval LST. So my original paperwork was scrapped and new paperwork was drawn up. The Air Force people at Kelly AFB in San Antonio definitely needed to upgrade their manuals.

Chapter 7: 6921ST SECURITY WING AND 6920TH SECURITY GROUP MISAWA AIR BASE, JAPAN 1972 - 1975

After we arrived at Misawa AB, Japan the first thing that my wife Maria said was "This place has a horrible smell". I myself didn't notice any foul odor or smell, but I guess after spending so much time in the Far East that the everyday smells of the different areas didn't bother me. We received temporary quarters at the Misawa billeting office and then started my in-processing the next day. When I entered the 6921st orderly room I was met by a couple of my previous tour's orderly room workers. They knew I was returning but a few were surprised to see me back at Misawa. While filling out my in processing paperwork a couple of my previous unit orderly room people told me that they had received my assignment paperwork, but thought it was a mistake. I was asked how the hell I was allowed back to Misawa. I informed them that I had straightened out my life and that I would not be seeing the First Sergeant or the Unit Commander about alcohol related incidents while I was assigned at Misawa this time around. The personnel specialist at the orderly room told me that I had been requested by name to be assigned to Trick 4 by Cecil who was my supervisor on my previous Misawa tour. This made me extremely happy.

While in billeting I was notified that our car would be arriving via a Navy LST at Hachinohe and I was scheduled to pick the car up. What a mistake it was that I brought that Volkswagen with us to Japan. The initial inspection, road taxes, car insurance and getting the car processed onto the base was a real pain in the ass. Not only that, I was risking my life every time I drove. Driving on the left-hand side of the road with my steering wheel also being on the left-hand side was pretty scary at times. It was always difficult to see on-coming traffic. I swore that on any of my future overseas assignments I would always buy a local car. I was also notified that my (1) hold baggage had arrived at Misawa.

Off-loading cars off Naval LST

Preparing my Karmann Gia to drive

The first time we departed the base via the main gate, I noticed a big change off to the left. The Stateside Snack Bar was no longer there. There was just the parking lot and the Pass and ID building. Misawa was also in the process of covering the benjo ditches on the main streets of the town. I don't remember how many times during the winter months that I had stepped into those snow-covered benjo ditches during my first tour at Misawa (nasty). I drove all over Misawa City and the outskirts of Misawa showing my wife the sites of the local area. She was not impressed. I later took her to the beach near Sabishiro and I pointed out to the east and told her to wave to her mother, sisters and brothers. That brought on the tears and she wanted to return to San Antonio, Texas. I convinced her to at least give Misawa a chance. Ginny was in a culture shock after arriving for her first time away from the United States and it took a while for her to get used to the local customs and daily way of life in Misawa. To top off the culture shock, she was from southern Texas where there is very little snow and the temperatures were much warmer. When the cold weather and snows hit northern Japan, she freaked out. By the end of January there was at least three feet of snow on the ground. Ginny had never been anywhere there were earthquakes. She of course freaked out the first time one of these earthquakes hit the Misawa area. I told her that they were frequent earthquakes annually. Some very strong and most are hardly noticeable. I told her she would get used to them. Of course she didn't believe me.

While accomplishing my in-processing on base I put my name onto the on-base housing waiting list. At that time there were three types of housing on base; trailer housing, CC housing and TOW (Time of War) housing. The worst of the three choices were the trailer housing which was located near the Q Gate and CC housing. In my opinion the best housing was TOW housing. Since I was only an E-4 and no kids the only on base housing list I was authorized to get on was the trailer and CC housing listing.

About three weeks later we found a one-bedroom house to rent on the outskirts of Misawa City. The house number was W-170D, which could be accessed via a dirt road and was next to a farmer's corn field. The base supplied all the furniture that we were allotted and we had our hold baggage we had shipped from San Antonio delivered to us. The refrigerator that the base supplied us had to be put in our bedroom because there was no room to put it in the living room/kitchen area. We had a kerosene-fed heating stove in living room/kitchen area and there was also the smell of kerosene throughout the house. The storage tanks for the kerosene were two 50 gallon barrels next to the outside wall of the house. I got a kick out of the kerosene storage containers in the "B" Battery area of Misawa. A lot of these houses were using Jet fuel pods (tanks) instead of the 50 gallon barrels. The property owners probably bought these jet fuel tanks at the Misawa Air Base Defense Reutilization & Marketing Service (DRMS) facility.

(1) Hold Baggage – A quick shipment of certain household items that was shipped and usually waiting for the Air Force member upon arrival at the member's new assignment. We were limited to 250 pounds

Our off-base house W-170

W-170 East of downtown Misawa on the highway towards Hachinohe

Japanese vendors of all sorts came to our off-base house trying to get me or my wife to buy their wares or work like sharpening knives and scissors. They would knock at the door and then let themselves into the mud room and call out to us. That was another thing that Ginny had to get used to.

Due to on-going training at Fort Meade, Maryland prior to arriving at Misawa, I was assigned to the Block 5 area on Trick 4. Cecil didn't let me work the new Block 5 position that I was trained to work. He said that the position was a waste of my talents, so he re-assigned me to be one of the section's controller billets. I was to be the supervisor of 14 people in the Activity Center 3 (AC-3) section. Cecil wanted a supervisor/operator not just an operator.

I had a great bunch of operators in my section which included our first woman operator. Initially I wondered if she would ever fit in with our group of male operators. Her nickname was Dixie and she proved to be a good operator and worked well with all her male counterparts. When softball season started she even beat out all her male counterparts when she turned out for the position of 2nd base on the Trick 4 softball team. Almost all the members in my AC-3 section worked hard for me at work and most of them liked to party hard too. Besides Cecil, who actually controlled the entire printer systems area in the operations building, a TSgt named Art and one of my counterparts whose name was Ralph controlled the work section next to mine. I coordinated with these two controllers on mission acquisitions and even though there was no official competition between our two sections we were constantly trying to out-do each other. Our sections were always battling for the number one spot in the unit's monthly report. All the Trick 4 printer systems sections, under the Cecil's guidance were consistently running first or second place out of the four operational tricks in all printer system mission objective areas.

My wife had to make several adjustments to her usual daily routines during her first year at Misawa. Initially she would try and stay up as long as she could when I worked the Mid shifts so we would both more or less get our sleep during the same time period. Since she didn't drive she was more or less stuck at the "W" housing area. Eventually she started hitching rides with some of the neighbors to go to the base or shopping in downtown Misawa. She would also sometimes walk to the POL Gate at the East end of the main base and caught a base bus that took her to the base facilities she wanted to visit.

Just after we arrived at Misawa I introduced Ginny to some of the mama-sans and josans that worked at the bars and clubs in AP alley. Initially, she could not help herself when she backed away from some of the josans or the mama-sans after my introduction to them. She couldn't stand the smell of the dried squid and/or fish on their breath and would back away from them. She didn't want to be rude and eventually got used to these smells. Almost all the josans and mama-sans took her under their wings and wanted to do just about everything for Ginny. Most of the Japanese she met mistook Ginny's nationality as being of the Philippine persuasion and on some occasions thought she was Japanese. She immediately became a good friend of

Masako who was the Mama-San of the Metro Bar at that time. Masako's house was also in the "W" area and within short walking distance from our house through the woods on a dirt back road.

Back road from W-170D to Masako's house, also in the "W" area

My wife and I attended our first Dawg Flight trip during one of the 72 hour breaks to Iwate-Ken Prefecture. Iwate-Ken is on the Northeast Coast of Honshu. This area has a very rugged coastline. We visited the Ryusendo Caves and a few other sights before returning to base.

Iwate-Ken Prefecture coast Line

Iwate-Ken Kitayamazaki National Park

Iwate-Ken entrance to Ryusendo Caves

The next Dawg Flight trip that we attended was a summer trip to the Ainu Indian village and the city of Sapporo on the northern Island of Hokkaido. We also visited the Sapporo Beer Factory and took the cable car to the top of Mount Moiwa. We spent the evenings having a few drinks in one of the bar areas of Sapporo.

Ainu Indian Village Museum

Ainu Indian Village Gift Shop

Sapporo Cable Car to Mt Moiwa

At the top of Mt Moiwa

Sapporo Covered Shopping Area

During this tour I didn't quit exploring the Misawa Machi. As a person left the main gate and turned left onto the main road and a right onto "B" Battery Road. (This intersection was close to the Misawa Police Station). As soon as you were on "B" Battery Road there was a dirt (or muddy) alley immediately on the right side of the road. I visited the Yae Bar in this alley quite often. One of the josans there was kind of weird, she liked to get her hand into your pants and pick off pubic hairs for her collection. She had several shot glasses on the back of the bar that were filled with the customer's pubic hairs. About a year later I was drinking at the Yae Bar and I was bothered by my drink having bits of hair in my drink. I found out that she had mixed the pubic hairs she had been saving with water and created ice cubes in the freezer for the customer's drinks. I told you that she was weird.

Catty corner to that dirt alley on the left side of the "B" Battery Road was a bar called the Balloon which I also visited quite often. Also across the street from the Balloon Bar on a street that ran parallel to the main street of Misawa was a bar that a girl by the name of Tomi (I think it was short for Tomiko) worked. She loved to knit things. Tomi knitted me two scarfs which were great to wear during the cold nights. On the back of the bar, nailed to the wall, was a knitted penis sock that held two hot glasses where a man's balls would have been located. This place was a must on my bar runs.

"Tomi"

During the winter of 1973 the base garage burned down. One of my people at work had his car being repaired at the garage when it burned down. It was a junk heap that he paid very little for. He made out like a bandit with the money he was awarded from the Air Force for losing his car in that fire.

Misawa AB had the Armed Forces Radio & Television Station (AFRTS) for anyone who wanted to listen to their radio programs or watch their limited Television programming. During this tour Misawa AB's Far East Network (FEN) showed old black and white programs like the Range Ryder, Lone Ranger, General Hospital and many others I can't think of at this time. I actually liked listening to some of the old radio programs they played in the evening like "The Shadow" than watch FEN's TV programs. I think we initially watched more local Japanese Television than the FEN's TV programs. Ginny got hooked on some of the Japanese soap operas.

At the intersection of the road that went to the POL Gate, there was a hole-in-the-wall restaurant called Kishiro's. This restaurant was number one on our places to eat at. The only drawback was that it was small and only about 10 people (that's pushing it) could get into Kishiro's at one time. So to have a chance at getting a seat in the place we always tried to go during the week instead of weekends. A place called Old Miyaki's located on the main street of Misawa and a Kobe Steak House called JuJu's were also other restaurants we often dined at. Our friend Masako's homemade boneless fried chicken, fried rice and gyoza's were Ginny's favorite. Masako is an outstanding cook.

Kishiro Restaurant

Our first out-of-town trip with our Volkswagen was to Towada City. I think that area was called Sanbongi before they gave the township the name of Towada City. Anyway, I wanted to take Ginny to the restaurant in Towada City called the Tijuana Pizza House. I wanted to show her how great the pizza house was set up with wooden tables with stumps for seats. The Ex-Air Force 292X1 was still working as a cook at Tijuana's. I didn't know this fact until my last tour at Misawa, in 1982, when I first met Rosie who ran the Stagger Inn in AP alley.

I usually ran the bars in Misawa after our last swing shifts, last day watches and maybe one evening during our 72-hour breaks. In addition I was more or less one of Trick 4's organizers for the "Roll Calls" we periodically held after the last Mid Shifts. I also organized the periodic Trick 4 "Roll Calls" after the last Day Watch's. We usually had our roll calls at the Metro, Florence, Toys or the Trick Bar. It was understood by most of the people on Trick 4 that if any damage occurred during of our roll calls that it would be taken care of by the individuals that were responsible. It was an agreement between the bar owners and us not to involve the base or Japanese police. Usually when the police did get involved in some of the incidents that sometimes occurred was because the police were actually in AP Alley when these incidents happened. Of all the roll calls I participated in I somehow lost all the photos of those roll calls. Wally, a good friend of mine, sent me a photo of a 1974 Sayonara roll call we had after a last day watch.

1974 Dawg Flight Sayonara Roll Call

Every year the Japanese farmers had a sled dragging competition just outside Misawa. Horses would try and drag these sleds over dirt mounds. They would literally beat these horses with wood sticks trying to get the horses to pull the sleds over these dirt mounds. Periodically some horses were killed during this competition.

Annual Horse sled dragging races on the outskirts of Misawa

Masako, the Metro Mama-san, introduced Katsue Obara to my wife. Obara-san owned the Sports shop next to the main gate and Katsue Obara owned the Venus Beauty Shop on the main street across from the Pass & ID parking lot. Obara-San loved to play golf at the Misawa AB golf course. During my last three tours at Misawa, Obara-San took me on several bar runs that mainly consisted of Saki Houses. I will never forget the one time that we went to this one Saki House near what I called the covered concrete alley. It was a two-story affair. We went to the top floor and ordered our sake. On the bar were the usual dried squid, pickled cucumbers, sushi and other assorted snacks. There was this one appetizer that looked grayish in color. It was nicely sliced and a couple of the Japanese customers sitting near this snack were picking up pieces of this meaty looking appetizer with their chop sticks, dipping the sliced meat into soy sauce and they seemed to enjoy the snack up until they asked the bartender what type of appetizer it was. The bartender answered with "Uma Chimpo", Japanese for horse penis. One of the customers ran to the toilet and the other looked amused. The bartender that served the "Uma Chimpo" told me that after the annual horse sled dragging competitions he would sometimes obtain the horse penis meat from the owners from the deceased horses. I never touched any type of unknown appetizer at that place after that episode.

Our next road trip out of Misawa was to Lake Towada. From Towada City the road followed the beautiful Oirase River valley to the Lake Towada National Park located in the Hakkoda mountain range. The winding road up to this old volcanic crater-lake is an impressive drive. While driving up the Towada National Park road that ran next to the Oirase River, there were several beautiful waterfalls. We stopped at the Oirase Gorge Water Falls (I think the name of the falls was Choshi falls) and took some photographs. I always stopped at this particular water falls whenever we drove that route up to Lake Towada. I later had a couple of the better pictures blown up into 8 X 10 photos and had both of them framed.

I finally was promoted to Staff Sergeant (E-5) on 01 August 1973. The promotion definitely helped us out financially. I still had the same responsibilities as a supervisor and operator at work.

One of my friends spent a lot of his off-duty time with us. Actually I think he adopted our place as his home away from home. His name was Myles and was of the Irish descent and from Pembroke, Massachusetts. Myles worked in the Block 5 section at work. He was single and resided on the second floor of Dorm 7 located at the Security Hill area. Ginny, Myles and I liked going to the Japanese theaters in Misawa with what everyone called "Combat Jugs" of Sapporo and bags of shelled peanuts. By the time the show we were watching got over there was always a pile of peanut husks on the theater floor. Myles also loved to go shopping. I myself hated shopping and felt out of place whenever going to Aomori or Hachinohe department stores. Myles and my wife always acted like little kids in a candy store whenever we went shopping at these department stores. Myles called his shopping trips "Stocking Stuffing Gift Shopping". Ginny treasured those shopping trips.

I always tried to invite co-workers and friends to Thanksgiving, Christmas and New Year's dinners. Also during this tour, we sponsored three big parties at our off and on-base residences. After each of these parties at our house, we always ended up running the bars of Misawa. Trick 4 usually had at least two catered parties at the Airmen's Club or the NCO Club each year. One of the parties was usually held in the September and October time frames and the other flight party was around the Christmas and New Year time frame. And as usual after these parties we usually ended up running the bars in downtown Misawa. I don't remember which Trick 4 Party this next incident happened after, but that doesn't really matter. During a Trick 4 Party at the club on base, our Flight Commander (We called him Captain Jack) hung out at the table that most of my co-workers were at. He danced with the wives and single women and we all were having a grand time at the party. When a bunch of us decided to leave the party and run the bars in downtown Misawa, Captain Jack asked if he could tag along with us. We had no problem with him tagging along with us. We ran the bars until about 3am and then decided to head back to the base. We had been carrying one of my co-workers (His name was Rick) and I had planned on taking him back to Dorm 7 on the hill in a taxi. Captain Jack told me that he could save me a trip to the hill by letting him take care of Rick. Since I was all partied out and tired, I didn't argue with him. What a big mistake that was. Rick was taken to Captain Jack's quarters and I won't go into all the details of what allegedly happened to Rick. Rick beat the hell out of Captain Jack. Captain Jack was admitted to the emergency room and Rick was arrested by the

Security Police. Early that same morning I received a telephone call from the Security Police. They told me to report to the Security Police station near the "S" curves road to the hill. With a serious hangover, I haphazardly wrote out a statement and Rick was released to our orderly room. There were several of us that made written character witness statements for Rick's court martial. Yea, the Air Force gave Rick a court martial.

What this Court Martial case boiled down to was an officer's word against an enlisted Airman's word. I was told that on the last day of the court martial the defense came up with new evidence. There was another officer that was at that time assigned at an Air Base in Taiwan. He had been caught and proved to be a homosexual and gave the Air Force OSI a list of names of his homosexual friends. Rick was found guilty of assaulting an Air Force officer and I think was given a General Discharge from the Air Force. I don't know what kind of discharge Captain Jack got, but he was also released from the Air Force. This incident has haunted me for a long time. I hope somehow that Rick overcame this horrible injustice and is doing ok for himself as a civilian. In July of 2012, Rick attended the Misawa Reunion in St Louis, Missouri. I found out that rick actually ended up with an Honorable Discharge. After he got out of the Air force he went to work for the Red Adair Corporation. He worked his way up through the ranks and became a worldwide consultant. He said the biggest job he had was putting out the oil well fires in Kuwait and Iraq. He resides in Houston Texas and I also think he has a home in Bermuda. He has done well for himself.

After living in W-170D for about a year and half, we were notified that we were finally selected to move onto Misawa Air Base family quarters. We moved into CC Housing, S848A2. Our on base housing was huge compared to where we were living in the "W" area of Misawa.

CC Housing S848A2

Ginny became more involved with the Base and off-base Catholic Church activities after we moved onto the base. The Catholic Priest at the downtown Misawa Church had been in Japan since the 1950's. His name is Father Andre and he was from Canada. The church on base worked closely with him and supported his downtown church and school in many ways. We have always kept in touch by mail with Father Andre since 1975. Ginny also got involved with punch pictures (This was a popular Japanese style art)

Father Andre at his downtown Misawa Church and School

My mother came to Misawa for a visit in 1974. We gave her the grand tour of Northern Japan. On one of our trips we took my mom, Chuck and his wife on the train to Aomori City and after visiting the Aomori Glass factory Ginny, my mom and Chuck's wife left Aomori with a bunch of boxed glassware. It looked like we had bought out the factory.

Aftermath of visiting the Aomori Glass Factory

South of Aomori there was a town called Asamushi. My mom wanted to buy a couple of the large glass fishing floats that she saw piled up near Asamushi. So we visited one of the fishermen and asked if it was possible to buy some of these glass floats. He said they were no longer using them because they were now using plastic floats and yes he was willing to sell the glass floats for 1,000 Yen a peace. We bought five and mom shipped two of them back to the states. I still have the three I bought.

Ginny and several other dependent wives visited some retired Catholic Nuns in the Northern city of Aomori. They were in Japan in the late 1930's and when war broke out between the United States and Japan they were put under house arrest. They could not preach their religion to any of the local community and their bibles were confiscated. I don't know if any of the nuns wrote about their exploits during their incarceration during our war with Japan but they definitely had some stories to tell.

Ralph was being cross-trained into another Air Force career field. That was just about the only way most of the USAF Security Service members could get stationed somewhere back in the states. We were in what the Air Force personnel system called an imbalanced AFSC. Anyway I decided to sell my Volkswagen to Ralph and Jan and bought a used car for the remainder of my tour at Misawa.

Besides the bars in AP Alley I frequented, I still continued to run the bars in other areas of Misawa City. During this particular tour I liked going to the Zero, New Yae and the Rich Bar in a two story complex of bars. The Amazon and 77 Bars on one of the back streets and occasionally went to the Honey Club on the main drag of town.

The Zero, Rich, & other Bars

The 77, Amazon other bars

Every year during the July and August months Misawa City and other nearby cities had a few great colorful festivals. They were the Tanabata Matsuri, Sansha Taisai Matsuri and the Aomori city Nebuta Matsuri. The parades were awesome and the street vendor foods were great.

The Misawa Sansha Taisai Matsuri

The Misawa Tanabata Matsuri (Star Festival)

On one of our trips out of Misawa took us west to Towada City. I looked for this place I was told about by the name of Tijuana Pizza House. The owner was originally from Italy and was married to a local Japanese woman. He later hired an ex-Air Force 292X1, whose first name was Rosie, as a trainee cook in this establishment. The pizza house was set up with wooden tables with stumps for seats. Unknown to me the Ex-Air Force 292X1 was working as a cook at Tijuana's. I didn't know this fact until my last tour at Misawa, in 1982, when I first met Rosie who ran the Stagger Inn in AP alley. I will tell you more about this guy in a later chapter of this book. Anyway the food was great, especially their pizza's.

Tijuana Pizza House in Towada City

I received my change of assignment orders during the summer of 1975 for the 6993rd Security Squadron in San Antonio, Texas. Before we departed Misawa we **went to** Towada City and had lunch at the Tijuana Pizza House. So it was back to San Antonio and home for my wife Ginny.

Chapter 8: 6993RD SECURITY SQUADRONKELLY AFB SAN ANTONIO, TEXAS 1975 - 1976

Before reporting for duty at Kelly AFB, Texas we visited my dad and mom. During the visit there was a small family reunion near Concrete, Washington at my Uncle and Aunts place.

My uncle had a bonfire and a grill set up for boiling crabs for the crab feed. It was the first time my wife had ever eaten crab meat. She loved it of course. I bought a used 4-door Plymouth to use during this stateside assignment.

Uncle's home near North Cascade Pass Road

My wife's first crab feed

After the family get together near Concrete, a met up with a friend of mine in my home town. He had a pilot's license and owned his own plane. He offered us a plane ride to Mt Rainier and around the local Kitsap County area. We accepted of course and got some nice photographs. The only other event that happened while on leave at home was a ride around Puget Sound on my dad's boat. He had an old wooden boat that slept four people. The boat also had a small kitchen and of course a small toilet area.

My Friends private plane

View of Mt Rainier at sunset

My Dad's Boat

My wife and my mother

On our road trip to San Antonio, Texas we stopped by Beal AFB, California to visit with my friend Ralph and his wife who had bought my Karmann Gia when they were transferred to Beal AFB. Ralph's new career change job was working on the electronic systems of the SR-71 Blackbird aircraft. The next stop before arriving in San Antonio was Phoenix, Arizona where we visited with my wife's uncle and aunt. When we arrived in San Antonio, my wife's family was extremely happy to see her back in her hometown again. My wife spent a lot of time with her family and friends while I was at work.

While processing onto Kelly AFB, the base housing office had me fill out a form which one of the questions was "What was I willing to pay a month for rent." I wrote down the amount of $200.00. When the base housing office person read what amount of money I was willing to pay he laughed and said he didn't have anything available in that price range. My wife said she knew better and mentioned where we had lived in 1971. We decided to rent at the Highland Apartments. We rented a duplex apartment which was located on East Southcross Avenue. The apartment was just three apartments down from the last place we lived in during my last assignment to San Antonio and the rent was exactly $200.00 a month.

When I reported to my duty section located at the Medina Annex operations facility I was not given any supervisory position because there were several Army and Airforce members that outranked me. So I was just another Printer Systems Intercept Operator which suited me just fine. The section I was assigned to was the same section I had previously worked in during my 1970 – 1972 tour at the Medina Annex.

During a period I wasn't at work, we drove to Gulfport, Mississippi to visit my wife's brother and his family. We also visited friends that we were stationed with at Misawa AB, Japan. They were both stationed at Keesler AFB, Mississippi at that time.

We drove to San Angelo, Texas during our 1975 Christmas and 1976 New Year period to visit with friends that we were stationed with at Misawa AB, Japan. They bought a home in San Angelo after he retired from the Air Force.

At work I met this guy by the name of Phil that worked in the Tape Library located in the operations building. We became good friends and I convinced him that he should request a transfer to Misawa AB, Japan. I told him that I had already requested my transfer back to Misawa AB. He had never been to Japan and at first he wasn't really interested in going there. I, of course, told him all about downtown Misawa and all the interesting places to see. I also told him about the annual festivals that were held every year in Misawa and other cities. I convinced him about requesting Misawa AB, Japan and I think he fell in love with the place because he eventually spent four tours there.

The summer of 1976 I visited two places. The first one was to Guernsey, Wyoming. I wanted to show my wife where I spent my childhood. I introduced her to the Green Family in Guernsey and showed her from a distance the log cabin we lived in at a place locally called Kelly's Park on the Platte River. Then I showed her Register Cliff and the petrified wagon wheel ruts caused by heavy loaded covered wagons making their way west on the Oregon Trail. These were located outside of Guernsey. I also took her to see what was left of Fort Laramie.

Kelly's Park on the Platte River

Log cabin we used to live in at Kelly's Park

Oregon Trail wagon ruts

During the spring of 1976 Phil and I were both notified that our next assignment was at Misawa AB, Japan. Believe it or not my wife was thrilled about going back to Misawa and looking forward to seeing her Japanese friends again. Phil was arriving at Misawa about three months after we arrived there.

My last road trip was to Jacksonville, Illinois during May of 1976 to visit my friend Vinny and his wife that we knew previously in Misawa, Japan. During our visit they took us to Springfield, Illinois to see Abraham Lincoln's tomb and his home. Vinny also took me to a friend of his that owned a farm. On this farm was a large pond. Vinny and the farmer asked me if I wanted to gig for bull frogs. I had never done this so I agreed. I had never eaten frog legs before and found that the frog legs tasted pretty good.

Lincoln's Tomb in Springfield, Illinois

Gigging for bull frogs

We had our hold baggage and household goods packed and shipped to Japan. We then moved in with a good friend of my wife. My wife didn't go with me to Japan, but arrived four months later. She wasn't ready to leave San Antonio and her family. She also wanted to visit friends and her brother in California. So at the end of July 1976 I departed San Antonio and flew to Japan.

Chapter 9: 6920TH SECURITY WING AND ELECTRONIC SECURITY GROUP MISAWA AB, JAPAN 1976 - 1979

During this tour at Misawa I arrived initially unaccompanied. My wife arrived 4 months later.

I decided that we should live closer to the Misawa City center. This time I looked for a house to rent in the "F" area of Misawa City and I selected F-408 to be our temporary rental home off base. I only hoped my wife would like it. During my last tour at Misawa we unfortunately had an American bought Volkswagen. Learning by my previous Misawa tour mistake I made the decision to buy a two year old used Toyota. What a difference that made in a much easier and safer drive in Northern Japan.

Misawa home F-408

I was again assigned to Trick 4 (also referred to as Dawg Flight) but this time Cecil was not my supervisor. He was now the Mission Supervisor of Dawg Flight. But Cecil told my new supervisor that he was getting me assigned to Dawg Flight. My new Senior Printer Systems Supervisor (SPSS) assigned me to (where else) the Activity Center Three section Supervisor billet.

A few months after I returned to Misawa, Phil arrived for his first Misawa tour. I had already convinced Cecil and my SPSS to get Phil assigned to Dawg Flight and in my Activity Center. I trained Phil in on his responsibilities as an Activity Center Three controller.

Of course I would have been remiss if I hadn't showed Phil around the local Misawa bars and clubs. He loved the Misawa nightlife, after last mid shifts and last day watch roll calls. We also ran the bars outside of AP Alley together on a regular basis.

Six months after arriving back at Misawa, we were offered a two-story duplex house in the TOW housing area near the main gate and we agreed to move in. The house number was S-370B. Since we spent a lot of time in Misawa City we did not have very far to walk to the main gate.

Base TOW Housing S370B

During this tour my wife and I attended three Dawg Flight Christmas parties. At the first Christmas Party we attended I was given a wooden Tanuki statue which represented the Machi Nezumi (Town Rat) award. This award was given to the Dawg Flight member who spent the most time and money running the bars of Misawa city. The statue of the Tanuki was made to look like a Japanese raccoon-like animal that held a bottle of Saki in one hand and a bar-bill ledger in the other hand. I was awarded the town rat award twice during this tour and I still have this prestigious Tanuki statues.

Tanuki statues for the Machi Nezumi awards

After our last day watches and during our 72 hour breaks from work I attended just about all the Dawg Flight Bar Runs in AP Alley. Some of us would continue the bar runs out of AP Alley and into the local Misawa Japanese bars and I usually left the group and run the remaining bars on my own. The following photos are just a few of the bars runs I was on.

Co-workers at the Companion Bar

Co-workers on a bar run

Bar hopping in AP Alley

Running the bars in AP Alley with my co-workers

During this tour my wife was again very involved with the base Catholic Church and in Father Andre's local Misawa City Catholic Church activities. In addition to our Dawg Flight parties, we also attended the annual Catholic group's Christmas parties.

During one of our 72 hour breaks during the summer, I had been partying with several of the people from work. I returned to our house on base just before sunrise. I tried to sleep on the couch in our living room, but everything seemed to be spinning around and around and it seemed to be horribly hot in the house. I unknowingly decided to go outside the house to cool off. I even turned on the water spigot with a hose attached at the side of the house to get some cold water on me. I gave myself a shower with the hose and then passed out on the lawn. I have no recollection of doing this of course. Anyway one of the neighbors called the Security Police. The Security Police arrived and woke Ginny up and then they assisted me into the house and into my bed. I knew both of the Security policemen and luckily they never officially reported the incident. My wife, of course, was embarrassed and pissed off at me. When I went to work on the first swing shift after this incident, there was a cartoon drawn of me taking an outside shower with no cloths on at one of the operation floor bulletin boards. Just like the bar girls in Misawa, everyone on Dawg Flight seemed to hear about or know about everything that occurred on and off-base.

My Japanese friend Obara-san liked to play golf on base and hunt pheasants near the rice fields in and around Aomori Prefecture. He also had several of his shot pheasants stuffed and mounted. He gave us one of his mounted pheasants. I really enjoyed having it displayed in our living room.

Stuffed mounted Pheasant

During 1977 Dawg Flight had a trip to the Snow Festival in Sapporo. My wife didn't want to freeze her ass off running around Sapporo so I went without her. We visited all the outstanding snow and Ice sculptures during the day and night hours and took a lot of pictures. The evening hours were spent eating at Shakey's Pizza and a few other restaurants and running the bars till the wee hours of each morning.

Sapporo City Snow Sculptures

Sapporo City at night

Sapporo's Shakey's Pizza

On 16 May 1978 while working a Day Watch, I was standing in the middle area of Activity Center Three, drinking coffee and bullshitting with a couple of the people that worked for me.

I was telling them that it was exactly 10 years to the day that Misawa last had a very strong damaging earthquake. No sooner that I had finished with my story the operations building started shaking. The floor starting jerking violently, unbolting some of our work positions from the floor. I was yelling at everyone to stay calm and to get between our work positions. No sooner than I headed for the main aisle, part of one of the air conditioning ducts crashed down onto where I had just been standing. That is when I told everyone to head for the nearest exit doors. Cecil and I ran around shutting down all the power circuit breakers in our area. Believe it or not after we turned the power back on and followed standard procedures for recovery, we were able to get all but two of our work positions back in operation. When this earthquake hit, my wife was in the upstairs bedroom of our on base house. She said that when the earthquake hit, she thought she only hit about three steps going down the stairs and was outside of the house in just seconds. We were hit with several aftershocks during the days that followed the initial earthquake.

We traveled by car several times to the cities of Towada, Hirosaki, Asamushi, Aomori, Hachenohe and to Lake Towada during this tour for shopping and sightseeing. We took a lot of photographs of course. One of the summers during this tour several of us on Dawg Flight went to Towada City to watch a Sumo exhibition or Junket. I had been following Sumo tournaments since my first tour at Misawa. I even got to meet wrestler's Jessie Takamiyama and Chiyonofuji.

Wrestling Ring (dohyo) for this Junket

Takamiyama is third & Chiyonofuji last

Jesse Takamiyama doing his thing at the Towada City sumo wrestling junket

Starting on my second tour at Misawa a bunch of us participated in Sumo Tournament Gambling at the Relax Bar in AP Alley. Before each tournament those participating would select 10 wrestlers who they thought would have the most wins during the 15 day tournament. The cost to play was 1,000 Yen. Whoever had the most wins at the end of the tournament won the prize money? Actually I think there were 1st, 2nd and 3rd place winners. We had similar games at work and at the Companion Bar.

**Relax Bar where we watched
Sumo Tournaments on TV**

During one of the summers Dawg Flight had a sightseeing trip to Hakadate. I had already been there several times before and wanted to show my wife that part of Japan. We of course took the ferry from Aomori to Hakadate. My wife couldn't get over the toilets on board the ferry. Not only was she to squat over the toilet she kept having to grab the different hand rails on the walls so she would fall over when the ferry moved from side to side in the roof seas. After checking into the hotel we were told about the two day itinerary for visiting the local sights. After the briefing several of us took the cable car to the top of Mt Hakadate to see the panoramic view of the city. During the nighttime hours I was elected as guide for a small group of us since I already knew the bar areas quite well.

Ferry to the port city of Hakadate

Hakadate Harbor Fishing Fleet

Hakadate Trappistine Convent

Hakadate Harbor taken from Mt Hakadate

During the summer of 1978, Masako and friends helped my wife and one of the woman that worked for me get dressed into Japanese Kimonos for picture taking at our house on base.

My wife & Connie

My wife, Connie and Japanese friends

During 1979 the U.S. Air Force Security Service (USAFSS) was changed over or renamed the Electronic Security Command (ESC) and our operations at Misawa became the 6920th Electronic Security Group (ESG).

In November 1978 I received my PCS notification. This time my Air Force command was sending me to RAF Chicksands, England. My wife was excited about moving to England and of course very sad for leaving all her friends in Misawa. Also in November I also received a line number t to be promoted to Technical Sergeant (E-6) that was effective in September 1980, after I got to RAF Chicksands. Our very close friend Masako surprised us with a going away gift. She gave us a beautiful cherry wood Japanese table.

My wife and her Japanese Cherry wood Table

Chapter 10: 6950TH ELECTRONIC SECURITY GROUP RAF CHICKSANDS, ENGLAND 1979 - 1982

After arriving at Heathrow Airport in London, England my wife and I caught a special bus for the military that took us to RAF Chicksands, Bedfordshire. We checked into the base billeting where we spent about 3 weeks. While processing into this RAF Base I was informed that I was being assigned to Charlie Flight. I found and bought a used car that another Air Force family had for sale. They were being transferred to another station. To me the base looked like a college campus instead of a military installation.

Welcome folder given to us upon our arrival at RAF Chicksands

We found a semi-detached house on Aspen Avenue to rent in Bedford, which was about 10 miles northwest of the base. Unlike Misawa Japan, the base did not supply any furniture for us to use. I configured a love seat out of the large cardboard box that our temporary household goods were sent to us in. We used four large Japanese pillows to form a temporary comfortable fabricated love seat. We had to buy three transformers to switch from 220 volts to 110 volts for some of the kitchen appliances. We had to buy a refrigerator at the Base Exchange (BX). They installed a transformer in an open area at the bottom of the refrigerator before they delivered it. When the remainder of our household goods got delivered it included our TV which could be used with 110 or 220 volts. One of the first things I noticed about the house was there were no outside water faucets. Our landlord said that we could buy a kitchen sink faucet attachment at a local ironmongers shop. I found out that there was a tax on outside water faucets. The majority of the homes had no outside water faucets. So we ended up attaching a hose to the kitchen sink faucet so we could water the garden and wash the car.

Aspen Avenue in Bedford is where our rental house was located

Our semi-detached house (left side) in Bedford

Our landlord managed the Swan Hotel which was located on the Ouse River that flowed through Bedford.

The Swan Hotel in Bedford on the River Ouse

The River Ouse with the Swan Hotel in the Background

I normally drove the A600 from Bedford to the base and entered what we called the upper gate.

The sign for RAF Chicksands on the A600 Road

Welcome to the 6950th ESG sign

The familiar AN/FLR-9 Circular Arrayed Antenna was again what we utilized at work for our signals monitoring and direction finding requirements.

RAF Chicksands AN/FLR-9 Circular Arrayed Antenna

After starting work on Charlie Flight I was informed that I would be replacing the existing Senior Printer Systems Supervisor (SPSS). This was the first time I was given such a senior manager position. I was still at the rank of SSgt (E-5) but had a promotion line number for TSGT (E-6) with the effective date of 01 October 1980. They tried to always fill the SPSS billet with a MSGT (E-7) if it was at all possible. The Printer Systems and Morse Collection sections were smaller areas compared to the Misawa Operations. The Chicksands Operations building also had a section called the Joint Operations Center Chicksands (JOCC).

The Flit River ran through the base. Most of the base housing was on the lower half of the base and we had to cross a small bridge over the river to get to that part of the base housing area.

The River Flit

The River Flit that ran through RAF Chicksands

Midway through the base there is the Chicksands Priory and Abbey supposedly built in 1150. Like I said before, this base looked more like a college campus than a military base.

It is said that the ghost of a Nun, by the name of Rosetta, resided in the Priory.

Chicksands Priory and Abbey

Entrance to the Priory

Priory facing the River Flit

A portion of the Abbey

Rosetta's tomb – One can neither see in or out of the window

The nearest little town to the base was Shefford. You could get to Shefford by using both the upper and lower gates to the base. After departing the lower gate, you needed to turn left onto the Ampthill Road and you almost immediately entered Shefford. I only frequented two places in Shefford. I usually bought to-go Chinese dinners at the Red Sun Chinese Restaurant and spent some of break time evenings at the Black Swan Pub. I heard the pub is no longer called the Black Swan.

The Black Swan Pub in Shefford

The only pub I frequented in Bedford was the Clay Pot Pub which was about two or three blocks from where we were living. The pub is now called the Blue Bell. I wasn't treated badly, but the local people didn't seem to want to warm up to me. I wasn't used to not having lots of bars in alleys and building like in the Philippines and Japan. You could roll out of one bar and into another in the far eastern countries. In the United Kingdom, it seemed like there was a quite a bit of distance in between pubs. So I didn't go to very many pubs while stationed at RAF Chicksands. When I did go to a few Pubs it was usually by foot or taxi.

**The Clay Pot Pub which is now called
the Blue Bell Pub**

I didn't mean that I didn't party. Our flight had pub crawls in the city of Luton. What was great about these organized pub crawls was that a mini-bus took us to several popular pubs and back to the base after our pub crawl was over. There were also flight organized bus trips to and from Medieval Banquets. The one Medieval Banquet I attended was at the Hatfield House. I heard later that Warwick Castle and other places also had

Medieval/Elizabethan Banquets. The people working the medieval Banquets dressed up as people did back in the medieval days, there were wenches serving mead and we ate with our hands. The whole affair was quite noisy and everyone usually had a great time.

Hatfield House

After arriving at RAF Chicksands, I looked up a guy that I was stationed with in Misawa, Japan. His name was Conrad and his Japanese wife's name was Satchiko. Conrad worked in the day shop at work, so we were able to do a lot of sightseeing together when my 3 day break was in conjunction with a weekend. They had already been at the base for over a year and this was Conrad's second tour at RAF Chicksands. In the beginning we rode in his car when he took us to local attractions and we would go by train from Bedford to London. The train ride was only 45 minutes to London. I had seen enough of London when I was stationed in San Vito, Italy. So I wasn't really enthused about seeing the sights again, but my wife had never been to London, so I let her have her fun. We showed her the Tower of London, Madame Tussauds Wax Museum, Big Ben, the Changing of the guard at Buckingham Palace, Piccadilly Circus, Nelson's Column in Trafalgar Square and Windsor Castle. After two trips to London, I figured she had seen enough and we concentrated on visiting other places. She later went with friends to London to see stage plays on the west end.

Tower Bridge Tower of London

The Tower of London

There was a girl on Charlie Flight by the name of Jane that worked in the aisle across from my desk. She was a Russian Linguist. Anyway we became good friends and she was invited over to our house quite often for visits and dinners. My wife and Jane became close friends. Jane was living off base in a small village nearby called Biggleswade.

The base tour office had sponsored tours and a bus trip to Paris, France came about, and my wife really wanted to go to France. I disliked France because of how they treated me in 1965. I swore I would never go back, but my wife spoke a bit of French and she wanted to go. So we did. The Bus trip took us onto the ferry boat at Dover and then off-loaded in Calais, France. I don't think the British bus driver liked the French. He was always yelling at them out the bus window during the trip to and from Paris. We spent two days in Paris and took a boat tour on the river Seine. We visited the

Eiffel Tower, Champs-Elysees, Arc De Triomphe, Notre Dame Cathedral, the Louvre and the white Sacre-Coeur Basilica which was located at the highest point in Paris.

Tour boat ride on the Seine River

The Eiffel Tower

The Arc De Triomphe on Champs-Elysees

Notre Dame Cathedral at night

Eight months after we had moved into our rental home in Bedford we were notified that the base had a vacancy for us to move into. Our new residence on base was 866D Hoover Place. While living in Bedford my wife had made a close friendship with our landlord's wife Adele. They went shopping together and went out to lunch together quite often. Our friendship with our landlord didn't end when we moved onto the base.

Like Misawa AB, Japan, my wife got very involved with the Catholic Church group on base. They Catholic ladies group liked to occasionally have lunch at the Hare & Hounds pub in the Old Warden Village which was north of and not far from the base. My wife loved their French Onion Soup and homemade bread.

Hare & Hounds Pub in Old Warden

Just outside of the town of Bedford was the village of Elstow. The village contained a lot of very old buildings and homes. The most famous building was called the Moot Hall where John Bunyan held his meetings.

The Moot Hall in Elstow

Other buildings in Elstow Village

Like I said earlier, I wasn't too interested in visiting London. I loved doing road trips into the midland heart of England. We just about spent every three day break time on road trips. Villages and towns that were close to base where we shopped and visited quite often were Clophill Village, Ampthill Village, Meppershall Village, Ickleford Village and the towns of Bedford and Hitchen.

Ampthill Village Homes

Meppershall Village home

Town of Hitchin

St Mary's Church in Hitchin

The Old George Pub in Ickleford

Our car was spending a lot of time getting repaired, so when Conrad and Sachiko were being transferred back to a stateside assignment I offered to buy their two-door Opel. The Opel was very dependable during the remainder of our tour at RAF Chicksands.

Our two-door Opel

In December 1980 I had to take my pregnant wife into the base dispensary due to her water breaking. They told me that she had time enough to reach the RAF Lakenheath Hospital. I laid the passenger seat back as far as it would go and I rushed my wife all the way to RAF Lakenheath, praying all the way that she wouldn't have our baby while on the road. We had a baby girl and of course I was allowed to be with my wife during her delivery. The nurse congratulated me after the delivery by giving me a shot of whiskey. At the age of almost 36 years old I had my first and only child.

I had taken the NCO Academy Correspondence course while stationed in Japan. I figured this correspondence course would be all I needed towards promotions. In April 1981 I was called into the unit commander's office. He told me I had to attend the NCO Academy in residence at Goodfellow AFB in San Angelo, Texas. He wouldn't accept my correspondence course. His policy was all had to attend the NCO Academy in residence. So my wife and baby were required to support themselves, with help from her friends, while I was at our command's NCO Academy.

After returning from the NCO Academy, we started to expand our road trips to see different places of interest. We visited Woburn Abby, Warwick Castle, Belvoir Castle, Burghley house, Knebworth House and the Stow-On-The-Wold located in the rolling hills of the Cotswolds

Woburn Abbey in Bedfordshire

Warwick Castle in Warwickshire

Belvoir Castle in Lincolnshire

Burghley House in Lincolnshire

Knebworth House in Hertfordshire

The hills of the Cotswolds in Gloucestershire

Town of Stow-On-The Wold

Town of Stow-On-The-Wold in Gloucestershire

During the fall period of 1981 my wife and several ladies that belonged to the on-base Catholic Ladies Club traveled to Berchtesgaden, Germany for a religious retreat. While at the retreat my wife also visited Salzburg, Austria. While she was at the retreat, I took some leave so I could take care of our baby daughter.

In December 1981 I was notified that my next assignment would be Misawa AB, Japan. That was going to be my forth tour at Misawa. It felt like I was going back home. My wife went on a spending spree buying gifts for her family in Texas and friends in Japan. We ended up boxing up the gifts and mailing them to Texas and Japan. We sure couldn't carry all of the gifts with us during trip to the states and Japan. We said all our goodbyes to co-workers and friends at RAF Chicksands and departed in March 1982.

Chapter 11: 6920TH ELECTRONIC SECURITY GROUP MISAWA AB, JAPAN 1982 - 1985

After arriving at Misawa AB during April 1982 we checked into base billeting and started the in-processing requirements. The first thing I bought was a used two door Toyota. Then we started looking for an off-base house to initially reside in and decided on a house (R-417) outside the Air Base's "Q" gate.

My daughter in front of R-417 in Misawa City

Pete and Masako were married in 1980 while I was stationed at RAF Chicksands, England. They both were running the Companion Bar in AP Alley, so of course we had to chow down on Masako's boneless fried chicken and cheese gyozas during our first visit to the bars in AP Alley. During some of the days during our processing in period we went to Pete and Masako's home, which was also just outside the Base "Q" Gate and she cooked up meals for us. She instantly fell in love with our daughter and spoiled her endlessly.

Companion Bar in AP Alley

As I was driving to the hill for my first swing Shift at the operations building I saw the very familiar AN/FLR-9 Antenna. That antenna system was the backbone to almost all my USAFSS and ESC assignments. I was informed that I was again being assigned to Trick 4 (Dawg Flight). After working one cycle of work looking for somewhere to fit in, I was informed by the day shop that they were moving me to Trick 1 (Able Flight).The Day Shop wanted me to fill the Trick 1 Senior Printer Systems Supervisor (SPSS) billet. They moved the existing Able Flight SPSS to the Trick 1 Mission Supervisor billet. His name was Billy and we became good friends and just like myself he loved running the Misawa City bars. I guess they figured since I had filled the SPSS billet at RAF Chicksands, England that I had experience in that position.

During the first summer we attended all the Misawa City festivals with our daughter. She was enthralled with all the floats, dancers, music and of course she tried just about all the food that was available at the food stands.

Misawa City food stands during the summer festivals

July Misawa-Shi festival

July Misawa-Shi festival

July Misawa-Shi Festival

I didn't run the bars that often, like my previous three tours at Misawa AB. I participated in the occasional roll calls in AP Alley and in the every two month Sumo Pools at the Relax Bar in AP Alley. Once or twice a month I would do bar runs outside of AP Alley. I liked visiting my Japanese friends that I knew from my previous tours.

There was this Bar I rarely went to during my last tour that I visited once in a while in AP Alley during this tour named the"007". What intrigued me about this bar were the bottles of poisonous snakes that sat alongside the bottles of whiskeys. I had seen similar jars of snakes while in Korea. I never tried any of these ridiculous drinks in Korea or Japan. There were lots of people who dared drinking these poisonous drinks including a lot of brave or stupid military personnel. I think a glass of this concoction was called Godo Ichiban (not sure).

007 Bar in AP Alley

Jars of Poisonous Snakes

Six months after our arrival we were offered and we accepted a single unit TOW house on base. The house number was S-389 and I was extremely happy that it was very close to the base's main gate.

Our on-base house S-389

Just after we moved into our on base quarters an old friend of mine showed up at our front door. It was my old friend Dan that I worked and partied with on my first tour at Misawa. It seems that after his tour in Germany he got out of the Air Force. He then attended college at the University of Kansas. In 1978 he was selected to attend the University of Tokyo as an exchange student. He graduated in 1979 and started working as an English teacher for the Berlitz Schools of Languages in Tokyo. Dan hated the Tokyo area and in 1982 he requested to be transferred to Sapporo. While working in Sapporo Dan ran into Mr. Morita who was still running the tours for Misawa AB. So he took time off to visit Mr. Morita and myself in Misawa. The next time I got together with Dan was in 2005 while I attended a mini reunion with friends that had retired and stayed in Japan. Dan eventually retired and stayed in Sapporo until he made the decision to return back to the states in 2014. Including the four years he spent at Misawa while serving in the Air Force, Dan spent a total of40 years living in Japan.

I continued participating in Sumo Tournament Gambling at the Relax Bar in AP Alley. As always, before each tournament those participating would select 10 wrestlers who they thought would have the most wins during the 15 day tournament. The cost to play was 1,000 Yen. Whoever had the most wins at the end of the tournament won the prize money. Actually I think there were 1st, 2nd and 3rd place winners. There continued to be similar games at work and at the Companion Bar.

I had a co-worker at RAF Chicksands, England by the name of Jane that we were very close with. She loved to babysit our daughter when we attended parties. She was also transferred to Misawa about the same time we were and she was assigned to the same flight I was on. As in England she would babysit our daughter off and on when we needed her.

Jane and our daughter

In the 1972-1975 Misawa chapter of this book I mentioned that there was this 207X1 Morse Operator that had gotten out of the Air Force and went to work as a cook at the Tijuana Pizza house in Towada City. His name was Rosie and he started up his own business in AP Alley called the Stagger Inn. He also married the owner of the Flamingo Bar. Anyway the food and drinks at the Stagger Inn was great.

The Stagger Inn in AP Alley

The winter of 1983-84 broke all the Misawa snowfall records. A total snowfall for the winter period was 239.4 inches. The main roads on base were usually taken care of, but off-base it was a mess. It seemed that I was constantly shoveling the sidewalks and the snow that piled up behind my car. The snowplows always kindly left me a large pile of snow behind my car.

**Some of the snowfall we got during
the winter of 1983-84**

As many times that I had visited northern Honshu and Hokkaido cities and places of interest during my last 3 tours at Misawa, I mainly stuck to the Misawa vicinity during this tour. I did check out for the first time the beautiful Komaki Onsen Resort near the Furamaki Train station.

Misawa Komaki Onsen Resort

Misawa Komaki Onsen Resort

I was promoted to Master Sergeant (E-7) in November 1984 and at work I had lost all my E-5 and E-6 supervisors that I initially had when I started work on Able Flight. I had to use the most senior E-4 personnel I had available in each activity center. What was worse, I was required write everyone's performance reports. In addition to that, the group took away some of the first sergeants duties and passed on these duties to the flight supervisors. Which I ended up on several occasions getting woke up during the wee hours of the morning to come and get one or two of my people, take them to the hospital for blood tests and get them back to their dormitory. Then there were those follow-up reports. Anyway, ever since I arrived at Misawa AB and Able Flight I had been approached on several occasions to volunteer for this new Electronic Security Command (ESC) program called Comfy Cobalt. Since I had lost my senior supervisors to ESC's Ladylove and Comfy Cobalt programs I decided to jump ship and volunteered for the Comfy Cobalt Program. The question I had for headquarters was if I was accepted, wouldn't I violate the Air Force's Top-Cat program due to my present rank. Three weeks later I was notified that headquarters waived me on the Top-Cat program and I was accepted into the Comfy Cobalt program and was being sent to RAF Edzell, Scotland.

I wasn't sad about leaving my job at Misawa, but was very sad that I would be saying goodbye (probably for good) to our Japanese friends and of course some of my co-workers.

We departed Misawa late August of 1985 and I was looking forward to my new adventures in Scotland.

Chapter 12: DET 2 693RD ELECTRONIC SECURITY WING AND DET 2 6950TH ELECTRONIC SECURITY GROUP

RAF EDZELL, SCOTLAND 1985 - 1989

Our family arrived in England at Heathrow Airport in the month of September 1985, where we caught a follow-on flight to Aberdeen, Scotland. We were met at the airport by a guy I had been stationed with before. He was picking us up in the unit's utility van. After arriving at RAF Edzell we checked into the RAF Edzell lodging.

A couple of days later I accessed the Air Force detachment and met with the commanding officer and day shop effort personnel. One of the Government contractors at the detachment offered me and my family temporary housing at his big estate near Forfar which was about 14 miles south of the base. The village of Finavon is where his estate was located. The estate was called the Carriage House and at the south end of the estate was a separate three bedroom apartment that had a full kitchen, bathroom, and living room. It was a perfect temporary setup for us and we agreed upon his request to rent the apartment.

Finavon Carriage House near Forfar, Scotland

Finavon Carriage House near Forfar, Scotland

I bought an Austin Maxi HL for ¥1000.00 from a Navy Master Chief that was departing RAF Edzell. It turned out to be a very durable car during my four years in Scotland.

Our Austin Maxi

I was put into a special training program as the Space Operations Mission Director with a 3 man operational crew working a different kind of a shift cycle. We worked four 12 hour nights (9pm to 9am), four days of break time and then four 12 hour days (9am to 9pm) four days of break time and then started the cycle all over again. At one time I think there were 23 Air Force personnel assigned to the Air Force detachment, plus three government maintenance contractors. The rest of RAF Edzell operational facilities were manned by British National RAF and US Navy personnel. The type of work we accomplished at the detachment was nothing like the work I previously was trained for. Before I could officially take charge of my crew I had to certify on three different positions. I was told that I should be completely certified after approximately a year of training.

Overhead view of RAF Edzell and surrounding landscape.

This is photo is of both the Navy Operations building and our Detachment

We were notified in November that there was an on-base semi-detached house available if we wanted it. After inspecting the house we accepted it. We had our hold baggage and household goods delivered and moved into our new home. Our neighbors were an Air Force family that we knew from previous assignments.

The Street we lived on at RAF Edzell and the semi-detached house we live in

Soon after we moved onto the base our daughter turned 5 years old. Since there was no school on base we set her up in the Luthermuir Primary School in the village of Luthermuir. The base provided the daily transportation for the RAF Edzell children to and from the school.

Luthermuir Primary School in the village of Luthermuir

When departing the base main gate and turned right we entered a very picturesque drive towards the villages of Edzell and Fettercairn. Both villages had good looking arches before entering the villages.

Road signs for Edzell, Fettercairn and RAF Edzell

Langstracht Road outside the base

Edzell Village Arch

Fettercairn Village Arch

The only drinking establishments that I went to in Edzell Village were the Central Hotel bar and the Panmure Arms Hotel Bar in Edzell. I mainly went to the pubs and hotel bars in the larger towns of Montrose and Brechin. The local guys and gals were great to drink and hang out with. Since I didn't want to receive a DUI and get into big time trouble I was introduced to a private taxi cab driver who set me up with a great price. He would pick me and my drinking pal up at my house and drive us to Montrose. When we were finished with the pubs and hotels in Montrose we would call him and he would drive us to Brechin and at the end of the night pick us up and drive us back to the base. I used his service all four years I was stationed at RAF Edzell.

Montrose High Street

Downtown Brechin

When I got a new guy assigned to my crew we became very good friends. His name was Garry and he loved to hit the pubs and hotels with me. Garry also came to our house for some home cooked meals. He was single and lived in the barracks on base. His RAF military roommate was from Scotland.

On one of my 12 hour day shifts, I was told to report to our detachment commander. He informed me that he was concerned about me and Garry spending a lot of our off duty time partying with the locals. He said there was a need for us to have a low profile here at RAF Edzell. After passing this information onto Garry, we both basically said "You have got to be shitting me". We both agreed to ignore his implied order not to party with the local populace.

On a few of my 4 day breaks we sometimes liked to walk to the Edzell Village. There was a shortcut by crossing the River Esk on what the locals called the Shaken Brig. There was another nice walking area that was entered via what the locals called the Blue Door. The trail basically followed the Esk River and was quite beautiful and serene.

Walking Bridge over the River Esk
The locals call this bridge the Shaken Brig

Blue Door entrance to the walking trail
Next to the River Esk

When I was stationed at RAF Chicksands in England I really liked to visit Castles and stately homes. I was intrigued specifically with the history of the castles. I paid an entry fee and sometimes a parking fee at all of the places I visited. The first castle I visited after arriving at RAF Edzell was close by to the base and was called Glamis Castle. I paid the entrance fee as usual, but the lady taking my money asked me if I was interested in joining the Scottish National Trust. She explained that for a monthly payment of £5.00 a month I could enter all the Scotland National Trust sites without paying anything. I would also receive a copy of the Scotland National Trust magazine periodically. This sounded like a good deal to me and I joined the Scottish National Trust.

Glamis Castle, Angus

I found out from co-workers that I could open a bank account with the Bank of Scotland in Edzell Village. I created the works – Savings, Checking accounts and a Bank of Scotland Visa Card. Actually, at the age of 41, this was my first credit card. My travels, from that point on, were made a hell of lot easier within the entire United Kingdom.

My wife was into buying antiques. So, on my off-duty periods we would take road trips to different towns so she could look for and find different kinds of antique items. She bought most of our antique furniture at Taylor's Auction house in Montrose. During the summer months we would take the B974 road from Fettercairn to Banchory. From Banchory we would travel up the A93 to Aboyne and Ballater visiting antique shop plus other stores. We never visited these places during the winter due to the B974 road was usually closed due to heavy snows.

Closer to RAF Edzell, We liked to shop in Brechin, Arbroath and Kirremuir. I got all of my haircuts in Brechin from an Italian run barbershop. My wife did most of her non-antique shopping in Montrose.

The B974 Road from Fettercairn to Banchory

Arbroath Abbey ruins in Arbroath

The Statue of Peter Pan in Kirremuir. The Peter Pan creator was J.M. Barrie. He was born here and was buried here.

In Montrose we went to eat quite often at the Roo's Leap. Roo's Leap was owned and run by Mark and Helen Johnson. Mark was ex-Navy and Helen was a local girl from Montrose. Other places in Montrose we ate at were the Corner House and the George Hotel.

Roo's Leap Restaurant and Bar in Montrose

When Garry and I went on our pub crawls we usually went to about four places in Montrose before heading to Brechin. We usually went to the Market Arms pub first, then the Corner House Hotel Pub, the George Hotel Pub and the Anchor Pub. Then we usually took our taxi service to Brechin and usually started out at the Caledonian, and two others I can't remember their names and ending up at the Jolly's Hotel Pub. Before ending our night out we usually got Chinese food at a place across the street from Jolly's. We usually got the food to go and sat on the sidewalk edge eating our food.

During an early winter morning Garry was contacted by our day effort that they had some paperwork for him to sign. He decided to go early because he had other things planned. He departed his barracks wearing his Air Force artic parka with his hood covering his head. Just as he walked past the base post office the morning reveille started playing. He stopped, turned to face the flag and saluted. As he was in this position a seagull landed on top of his parka hood. Several people that were in the post office when reveille started were waiting for it to end. They all started laughing at Garry's predicament. While saluting, he moved his hand above his hood to scare off the seagull. The seagull flapped its wings and lifted temporarily and then resumed its perch on top of Garry's parka hood. Garry tried twice to scare away the seagull without success and then the Reveille ended with Garry flinging his hands and arms at the seagull and finally succeeding in scaring the seagull off. Garry's seagull encounter got around the base and everyone got a laugh out of Garry's antics with the seagull.

On one of our four day breaks Garry and I were invited by a couple of local friends that we drank with to attend a local soccer match in Montrose. We enjoyed the match and afterword hit a few pubs. About eight of us entered the Corner House hotel pub and we were a bit loud and having a good time when one of the guys told Garry and I that there was a guy sitting at the end of the bar really giving us the stare. Garry and I both looked at the same time and we both waved at our detachment commander. He got up and left. Just before our first night shift started Garry and I were both called into the detachment commander's office. As we stood before him, he said that we had completely disregarded what he had told us about keeping a low profile. He told me that he was having Garry transferred from my crew to another crew. He further urged us to drastically tone down our partying with the locals. After being dismissed and we were walking out his office door, Garry said "Not even Hitler would break up drinking buddies". I am sure our commander didn't like his comment. Even though we had been split up the both of us still kept going on pub crawls on our own and sometimes we were able to party together.

In December 1986 I had a heart attack and was rushed to the Stracathro Hospital near Brechin. I was stabilized and the Navy Base doctor requested that the hospital needed to get photos of my heart to find out what kind of damage was done to the heart. The hospital doctor that was taking care of me told the Navy doctor that I would be put on a waiting list to get this procedure done. The Navy Base doctor said that was unsatisfactory and he contacted his higher ups that he needed a medivac plane to pick me and my family up and fly me to Germany to get this procedure done as soon as possible. My wife, daughter and I were taken to the Dundee Airport in a Royal Marine ambulance. My family and I were loaded onto awaiting Medivac plane and we were flown to Wiesbaden AB, Germany. We were then transported by ambulance to Landstuhl Regional Medical Center. I was admitted and afterwards my wife and daughter were taken to base lodging. I was scheduled for the heart investigation procedure (I think they call it an angiogram) in a couple of days. Well there was a sudden opening for this procedure early the next day and of course my wife was unaware of this. When my wife and daughter came to visit me that morning they found that I wasn't in my room and asked the person that was cleaning the room where I was. The person told her "oh, he is gone" Talk about being freaked out. My wife was beside herself until a couple of nurses explained to her that I was in surgery getting the procedure done.

After the doctor studied the film from the procedure, he had the film for sent to Walter Reed Army Medical Center in the States for further analysis. While I was on bed rest my wife contacted a friend of hers that was stationed in Germany. Her friend picked my wife and daughter up and they spent time that they weren't spending with me. A couple of days later the medical staff injected me with something and had me walk on a treadmill. I was to walk until I could no longer do so. I actually was able to walk at a fast pace for about 10 minutes and then my legs gave way. Walter Reed Medical Center sent the doctor that attended me their recommendation. They recommended not to do open heart surgery. It seems that my aorta vein had a blockage and three veins were created circumventing the blockage. So he said for now I could continue my life normally, but there was still that chance that there was still the possibility that there would be a need to have open heart surgery done in the future.

When I was initially admitted into the Stracathro Hospital the Scottish doctor told me that I needed to quit smoking and watch what I was eating while living in Scotland. The Scots used pure lard in preparing most of their cooked meals. Well, I quit smoking and I cut back on my pub crawls but still consumed the Scottish food. I know I felt much better in the years following my heart attack and I am sure it was because I quit smoking cigarettes.

Stracathro Hospital near Brechin

After returning to my duties at the detachment I completed my training and became fully certified on all three positions and was awarded the Space Badge and adding to my Air Force Specialty Code (AFSC) the Special Experience Indicator (SEI) the 1ZA designation.

There was one of many pet peeves I had working at this small Air Force detachment. I wasn't interested in any of the so-called very important people (VIP) that visited our detachment. Our commander always wanted as many of us to gather with him to welcome these VIPs and it was usually at the Ramsay Arms Hotel in the Fettercairn. Every time I didn't show up for these gatherings our commander would jump in my shit and told me it was my responsibility as a senior NCO to attend these functions. As far as I was concerned, if he wanted to brown nose these VIPs he could have done it on his own. There were also enough day shop support people to attend these gatherings without dragging us shift workers into the picture.

Ramsay Arms Hotel in Fettercairn

In March 1987 the RAF Edzell Navy Catholic priest, Father Sadano, asked the Base Catholic Ladies Society if they were interested in traveling to Rome, Italy for an ordination ceremony he was attending and would they like a private audience with Pope John Paul II. My wife and several other wives definitely wanted to do this. So I ended up taking care of our daughter while she was gone. While in Rome, Father Sadano acted as a guide and showed the wives all the points of interest in Rome. The visit to the Vatican area and the private audience with the Pope was an experience my wife will never forget.

Our detachment commander was always pushing me to attend the Senior NCO Academy. I kept telling him over and over that I would never be promoted to E-8 or E-9 due to my overall conduct during my Air Force career. I had a lot of poor Airman Performance Reports during my career. There was no way I was going to get any more promotions and I don't think he gave me a favorable performance while he was our commander. He couldn't criticize my work ethics while on duty, but he sure criticized my off-duty activities.

RAF Edzell was involved in a United Kingdom wide NATO exercise. Unfortunately we had to participate. There were sand bag bunkers outside and inside our perimeter fence. The crew working didn't participate but those on their breaks and the day effort people were involved with the NATO exercise. For two nights in a row Garry and I huddled in one of the outside bunkers not seeing or hearing anything suspicious. On the third day we were attacked by low flying aircraft dropping a yellow smoke bomb making it a biological attack. We were supposed to don our gas masks. Garry and I didn't don our gas masks and ok we were dead now leave us alone.

We were super happy when it was over and the daily grind was back to normal.

Participating in the NATO Exercise

In the fall of 1987 Garry received his next assignment to Osan Air Base, South Korea and I was called into our detachment commander's office. He told me that the NCOIC of our sister detachment at Osan AB, Korea had a heart attack and was looking for assistance. He said he had selected me for the temporary duty. I told him I didn't want to go because I didn't want to be separated from my family for the three or four months that I was going to be at Osan AB. I knew it was a poor excuse because my military obligations override my being with my family. My excuse didn't hold water with him and he was still sending me. I had already planned a going away party for Garry at the Jolly's Hotel in Brechin. I had paid for a stripper that I hired out of Edinburgh to put on a show for Garry and of course us. I invited who I thought were good friends of Garry's and told them don't let our commander find out about this party. Our Director of Operations, who was a Captain, found out about the party and approached me asking if he could come. I said I sure hope his boss, the detachment commander, wasn't going to bring the hammer down on him for not telling him about the party. The Captain said he wasn't worried about it and he really wanted to attend this going away party. I thought this party was to only include our detachment people, but it didn't turn out that way. Seems the locals in Brechin got wind of our party and a bunch attended. Someone from the detachment took a video of the stripper and Garry. Garry sat in the middle of the dance floor on a chair and she proceeded to take all her clothes off while dancing around him and occasionally straddling him while he sat on the chair. It was a great going away party. The video was given to Garry as an additional going away present. Since I was leaving for Korea before him, he asked me to take the video with me and give it to him when he got to Korea.

My travel to Korea was one hell of a long trip. I flew from Aberdeen, Scotland to Heathrow, England. From Heathrow, England I flew to New York, then New York to St Louis, then St Louis to San Francisco, then San Francisco to Hawaii, then Hawaii to Tokyo and finally

Tokyo to Seoul, South Korea. After a taxi ride to Osan Air Base, I checked into the 6903rd Electronic Security Group orderly room where they assigned me a room in the NCO dormitory. The Detachment was separate from the main 6903rd operations building. I was introduced to the detachment commander who asked me if I wanted to work on one of the crews or the day shop effort. I selected to replace one of the crew supervisors and in turn the supervisor I replaced went to the day shop.

I went to the Skivvy 9 Lounge with my crew members after the first work shift. Skivvy 9 was the local nickname of the 6903rd Electronic Security Group. While getting to know my crew mates I told them about Garry coming to Osan and the video of his going away party. They said they would love to see the video and asked me to bring it to the lounge after our next work shift. After the next shift I brought the video to the Skivvy 9 lounge and played it on the lounge's TV. Not only did our crew enjoy the video, so did a lot of other people in the lounge. Garry became well known before he even arrived.

During my first break in work I went to the town outside the base's main gate with one of the guys on my crew. The name of the town was Songtan. I had been to Songtan on leave in 1969 for a couple of days, but really didn't get a chance to see all I could see. As we were hitting the bars and clubs on the main street, I ran into a good friend of mine that used to work for me in Misawa, Japan. His name was Chuck and he was married to a Korean Girl and lived in Songtan. So I spent a lot of my Osan AB temporary duty off time hours with him and of course Garry after he arrived. Chuck took me to Seoul and showed me around the bar districts there and of course showed me where the best bars were in Songtan. With my new knowledge of Songtan, I in turn showed Garry where the best places were to drink. I introduced Garry to this one Korean girl that worked behind the bar at this club I always went to. Her name was Choy and I didn't know that Garry had married Choy until several years after I retired.

My wife wanted me to buy s couple of blankets and a bunch of tennis shoes in different sizes for our daughter. So after buying a bunch of this stuff, I mailed the stuff off to Edzell, Scotland. The tennis shoes worked out great of course. After she outgrew one pair she had a larger size waiting to wear.

After returning from my temporary duty in Korea, I really needed a long rest, but had to get back into the work scene. On my four day breaks instead of pub crawls I travelled the roads of northern Scotland visiting different towns and of course castles.

The town of Pitlochry

The traffic on the main drag of Pitlochry

Bridge over Tay River near Aberfeldy

Sterling Castle

Wallace Monument in Sterling

Blair Castle in Perthsire

Town of Stonehaven

Dunnottar Castle ruins south of Stonehaven

During 1988 we had visitors from the states and RAF Chicksands. My dad and mom came to visit and friends of ours that were stationed at RAF Chicksands. We showed both of them around the local area and I think they had a great time.

Also our friend Jane who was stationed at RAF Chicksands when we were in Scotland called us and said that her sister Sue and her two kids were visiting and she wondered if we could meet them at Alton Towers in England. So I decided to take leave and drive south to the Alton Towers Resort located in Staffordshire, England. My daughter and Jane's sister's two kids really enjoyed the rides and other amusements. After we said our goodbyes, we decided to visit a few places while in northern England and during our drive back to RAF Edzell. The first place we visited was the Bamburgh Castle on the east coast of Northumberland, England and then we stopped at this place called the Preston Mill and Phantassie Doocot. Preston Mill was a very old water mill and the strange looking Doocot used to be used for pigeons. I read that during the winter months they ate a lot of pigeon pies to survive. Since then the majority of doocots in England and Scotland were tore down because the pigeons were ravaging the farmer's crops.

The last stop on our way back to RAF Edzell was a visit to the Scone Palace located just north of Perth.

Bamburgh Castle

Preston Mill

On one of our road trips we visited five castles in a two day period. These castles were all located in Aberdeenshire. The five we visited were Fraser Castle, Drum Castle, Fyvie Castle, Crathes Castle and Balmoral Castle.

Fraser Castle

Drum Castle

Fyvie Castle

Crathes Castle

Balmoral Castle

One evening I was socializing at the Market Arms pub in Montrose and was asking some questions about some of the castles in Scotland. I was telling them about the ones I had already visited. They all agreed that I knew more about the castles of Scotland than they did. None of them had visited any of the castles I had and they only knew about the ones closest to Montrose. That was surprising to me. If I had grown up in Scotland I think I would have travel far and wide to visit these castles.

I imagine you are wondering how on earth was I able to get all the time off to take these road trips and visit all these towns and castles. I worked four 12 hour night shifts, got four days off, and then worked four 12 hour day shifts. I would take leave for one of those four day shifts and be off-duty for 12 days. This allowed my family and me to do a lot of traveling. Plus the fact I had a lot of leave time accrued that I could take. My next big road trip was towards the Isle of Sky. We drove up to Inverness, then along Loch Ness, then past loch Cluanie. While driving past Loch Cluanie there was a Scotsman playing his bagpipe and selling heather seeds at a scenic pullover. We then drove through Glen Coe and ending up at the Eilean Donan Castle on Loch Duich. We decided not to go to the Isle of Sky and returned back to RAF Edzell.

Urquhart Castle remains on Loch Ness

Bagpiper selling heather seeds

Road through Glen Coe

Eilean Donan Castle on Loch Duich

When the personnel at the detachment heard that our commander was being replaced the majority of us were extremely happy that he would be out of our lives. When I was told that I was required to go to the change of command ceremony I ignored the requirement. About a week later I was called into the new commander's office. He told me to shut the door and sit down. He proceeded to tell me all the things that the previous commander had passed on to him about me. He told me that he had also talked to all the technicians and day effort people and they all said I loved to associate with the locals and achieved all that was required of me while on duty. He told me that as far as he was concerned whatever was passed onto him from the previous commander was being disregarded by him. He told me to keep up the good work and feel free to confide in him about anything. He had an open door policy for all his people. Finally – A personnel friendly commander. Also later the director of operations told me about the things that the previous commander had told him about me. Man was I glad to get that idiot out of my life.

I could keep showing you pictures of other castles that we visited, but I will just pass on to you the names of these other places: Craigievar Castle in Aberdeenshire, Menzies Castle near Aberfeldy in Perthshire, Culzean Castle in Ayrshire, Inveraray Castle on Loch Fyne in Argyll along with the Inveraray Jail. The 1820 to 1889 Inveraray Jail consisted of three floors overlooking Loch Fyne and had a lot interesting tales about the prisoners.

I was notified that my last assignment, before retiring from the Air Force, was working in the ADF at Buckley AFB, Colorado. So we wanted to see a few more places and visit and say goodbye to some good friends in Bedford, England, But before we took that trip to Bedford I wanted to do something that a friend of mine at the Corner House in Montrose had offered me. He was actually the son of the owner of the Corner House. He was a pilot for the British Airways and had his own private single engine Cessna aircraft that he flew out of Dundee. He had offered me a ride in his plane to fly over the area and over the base if I wanted to. I had always wanted to take a bunch of photographs from his plane of the local area around Edzell. So first I asked my Captain if I needed to tell anyone that I was going to be doing some low level flyovers of the base taking photos. He said that he thought the Edzell RAF Commander needed to be contacted for approval. The Captain said he would take my request to the RAF Commander. Not wanting to wait for the approval I then set up a date and time with my friend for this flight. A day effort friend of mine by the name of Dennis also wanted to go with me and my friend at the corner house agreed to also take him up with us. Dennis had never flown in a small plane before and at the end of our flight he said he would never fly in a small plane again, but he was happy to get some great photos. The day that we flew around the area it was very windy and it was kind of a rough ride. When trying to land at the airport in Dundee the pilot was coming towards the landing strip sideways due to the strong gusts of wind that he was facing. Dennis didn't understand why we were coming in sideways. I told Dennis that the pilot was facing the wind and just before landing he would straiten the plane out to land. Just as we were to land the plane was straightened out and then a real strong gust of wind tipped the left plane wing towards the runway and the pilot gunned the engine and came around to try landing again. Dennis was white as a sheet. We landed safely of course on the second try.

Unknown to me, that when we were doing our low level flights over the base, the RAF Commander was giving some visitors a tour of the base. One of the visitors asked about the low flying aircraft over the base. The RAF Commander said he knew nothing about us. Turns out that my Captain forgot to tell the RAF Commander about us doing the low level flyovers. The Captain and I end up having to report to the base RAF Commander. The Captain told the RAF Commander that it was his fault for now informing him of my impending flyovers. What the RAF Commander requested from me a week later was that he wanted copies of my photographs which I gladly gave him.

A couple of photographs I took of my work place on RAF Edzell

There were only two golf courses I golfed at while stationed at RAF Edzell. I mostly golfed at the public course just outside of Brechin. I did golf at the public links course in Montrose a few times. I wanted to golf at the St Andrews golf course, but never did, but we visited the town of St. Andrews and its famous golf course. After there was change of command at our detachment the new commander organized a golf tournament for those interested with a lunch gathering after the tournament. I actually took first place and was given a trophy. I am not that great at playing the game of golf. The guys at the detachment must not have been that great at playing golf for me to take first place.

My daughter liked to watch the cartoon series Thomas the Tank Engine on the BBC channel. So we decided to give her a ride on a real railway car pulled by a steam engine. There is a 10 mile preserved railroad setup between Aviemore to Broomhill via the Boat of Garten. It was called the Strathspey Railway. Not too long of a ride but my daughter enjoyed the ride and shopping afterwards.

Strathspey Railway using old steam engines to pull the railcars

I took a two week leave and we headed south. Our first stop was at the Drumlanrig Castle in Dumfries shire in southern Scotland. From there we travelled to the walled city of Chester, England. The beautiful City of Chester is on the River Dee and was called the Gateway to Wales.

The beautiful city of downtown Chester

Walled City of Chester

From the city of Chester we entered Wales and continued on to Snowdonia National Park where we stopped and viewed the Swallow Falls and got some pub grub.

Snowdonia National Park

Swallow Falls in the Snowdonia National Park

We left the National Park and traveled to the Conwy Castle. After sightseeing we checked into a local bed and breakfast facility. The next morning we headed across a bridge to the Welsh Isle of Anglesey where we visited the longest name of a town in the world. I am not going to attempt to type it up. I took a photograph of the name of the town. From what I read on a brochure the town name translated to "The church of St Mary in the hollow of white hazel trees near the rapid whirlpool by St. Tysilio's of the red cave".

The Welsh Town with the world's longest name

The next two places we visited in Wales were the Caernarfon Castle and Chirk Castle.

Caernarfon Castle

Chirk Castle

After staying at another bed and breakfast near the Chirk Castle we departed Wales and headed for Stratford-Upon-Avon in England where we visited the William Shakespeare exhibit.

Stratford-Upon-Avon River

William Shakespeare visitor center

After visiting Stratford-Upon-Avon we headed for our final destination of this road trip. We checked into a hotel and called our good friends that lived in Bedford. We were invited to dinner at the Swan Hotel in Bedford with sweets and coffee afterwards in the lounge area. Mr. Zhodi gave me a bottle of Glenlivet Malt Whiskey as a going away gift. They also paid for our dinner at the Swan Hotel. We said our goodbyes and my wife cried of course when we started back to Scotland the fastest way possible which was on the main motorways. We did stop at the Moffat woolen mill to buy some sweaters.

The Zhodi Family

The Ballew and Zhodi gals

During our last month at RAF Edzell, we had our household goods packed and shipped to Denver Colorado. We visited our local Scottish friends and said our goodbyes. We had a nice going away diner at the Corner House in Montrose and the ladies there gave my wife a going away present. We checked into the temporary lodging on base and when it came time to depart the base, we were driven to the Aberdeen Airport in the detachments utility van. From there it was flights to Heathrow Airport and the states.

Our good bye to the Corner House staff

Chapter 13: AEROSPACE DATA FACILITY, DET-3 HEADQUARTERS SPACE SYSTEMS DIVISION
BUCKLEY AFB AURORA, COLORADO
1989 – 1991

ADF Det-3 Headquarters Space Systems Division

Ground level view the ADF Det-3 facing towards the Rockies

I took some leave time and we visited my wife's family and friends in San Antonio, Texas. While there I bought a new Ford Aerostar Van. After a short visit with everyone we drove to Colorado. We checked into Lowry AFB temporary housing and sort of started my in-processing at the base. It seems I had to deal with Fort Mead, Maryland for all my personnel and pay matters. At Lowry AFB the personnel office told me to report to the ADF at Buckley and they would be the organization to really process me into their operations program. On my assignment orders there was only coded letters instead of the name of the organization I was being transferred to. I found out that I was being assigned to the Aerospace Data Facility (ADF), Detachment-3. Located at this facility was also the Headquarters Space Systems Division (SSD). I processed in with where I was going to work at the ADF and they gave me time to find a house to rent before I actually started working there.

It did not take us long to find a house to rent and our household goods delivered. We rented a house in Aurora that was close to Buckley AFB and got our daughter enrolled into school. No sooner than we were getting settled in we were hit with a lot of snow. Welcome to Colorado.

First snow of the year and wishing I had a snow blower

When I finally reported for my first work period I was introduced to my new supervisor which was a civilian. He said that my work position and duty title was to be as a Senior Multi-Mode Systems Operator/Analyst. Another operator, who had been at the ADF for a couple of years, was assigned to train me in on the operations of this position. I was also informed that I would be writing my trainer's Airman Performance Reports since he was an E-4 Sergeant. My trainer was very knowledgeable of the position and the mission and it did not take me long to learn everything I needed to know to work the position on my own.

At the Lowry AFB personnel office I informed them that I wanted to retire from the Air Force in January 1991. They said they would report my request to Fort Meade, Maryland. My request came back approved of course. So from that point on I did my job at work and during my off-duty times I experienced life in the region of the Rocky Mountains.

In October 1964 my best friend Bruce was about to enter the Air Force. My entry date into the Air Force wasn't until December. We got together before he left for boot camp in San Antonio, Texas. I took a five dollar bill and cut it in half. I gave him one half and I kept the other half. I told Bruce that the next time we got together we were going to buy a bottle of whiskey and celebrate our reunion. After arriving in Colorado in 1989 I found out that Bruce was stationed at the Air Force Academy in Colorado Springs, Colorado. His mom gave me his telephone number and I called him. He drove to my house and after 25 years we were finally reunited. We both actually still had our halves of the five dollar

Bill. Unfortunately $5.00 did not buy a bottle of whiskey so we both still have the two halves of the five dollar bill.

After 25 Years we still had the two halves of the five dollar bill

I found out that Bruce was also retiring the same time I was. But before we retire Bruce wanted to take me Elk hunting and some ice fishing. I had hunted for deer and elk with my dad, but never did any ice fishing.

I took my wife and daughter out to eat breakfast and the IHOP restaurant in Aurora one morning. As we were eating our breakfast my wife said that there was a guy starring at us. He was sitting in another booth catty corner from us. I looked his way and he waved and acknowledged my look at him. He finished his breakfast while we were still eating ours and came over to our booth. He asked if I remembered him. I told him that I couldn't put a name to his face. He said that he was my cell mate in the Misawa Correctional Facility. What a shock. After all these years I run into a guy I had only met in a jail cell.

Bruce called me and told me he was going ice fishing near the town of Cripple Creek. He wanted me to go with him. Since I had never done ice fishing I told him I would like to go with him. I enjoyed being together with Bruce, but can't say the same about ice fishing. I like fishing in mountain streams and lakes during the warmer months. While we drilled holes in the ice Bruce asked me if I wanted to go hunting for elk a few months before we retired and I told him yes. I later called my dad and mom and asked them if they were coming to Colorado to visit us during the summer of 1990. They said yes. So I asked my dad if he would bring the 30-30 and 30-06 rifles with them when they visited us.

Ice fishing on a lake near the town of Cripple Creek

During June we visited the old mining towns of Victor, Cripple Creek and the Red Rocks Park and Amphitheatre. We also visited Golden Colorado.

Cripple Creek, Colorado

Golden, Colorado

My dad and mom arrived for a visit and as promised, he brought my rifles. While visiting us my mom and dad told us that they wanted to visit friends in Guernsey, Wyoming. So I offered to use our van to travel to Guernsey and they agreed. I took some leave and all five of us took off on our road trip to Guernsey. The last time I was stationed at Kelly AFB in San Antonio, Texas we travelled to Guernsey to visit friends and show my wife the old log cabin we lived in next to the Platte River. This time I was going to show my daughter the same old log cabin we lived in.

Dad and mom also wanted to check their old place too. When we arrived at Kelly's Park the old log cabin was gone and a nice new log cabin had been built close to where the old structure was.

The people that lived in the new cabin invited us in for coffee and snacks. While my mom and dad were visiting with the people, I took my wife and daughter for a walk near the river and up towards the cliffs that had a couple of caves that my brother and I used to play in.

New cabin next to the Platte River

Cliff caves my brother& I played in

I also wanted to show my wife and daughter Fort Bridger, Wyoming. So we traveled west on I-80 and visited Fort Bridger.

The replica of old Fort Bridger & there were also newer structures at the fort

After my dad and mom went back to their home I called Bruce and told him that I had received my two rifles. He told me to bring them to Colorado Springs and he would take me to the Air Force Academy's firing range. His friend worked at the range. On my next off-duty day I went with Bruce to the firing range. I tried to get the best sight alignment as I could with both rifles. The results on my targets were good enough for me. After leaving the Air Force Academy Bruce started planning our hunting trip for elk. He was going to use his Jeep and a luggage trailer to haul all the gear and extra gas. I told him that he should take care of everything and I will just show up when the time comes. If he needed any cash or items he didn't have for the trip to let me know and I would supply them.

In the fall of 1990 I went hunting elk with Bruce and his friend. We drove to the southwest portion of Colorado near the small town of Saguache which was just east of Telluride, Colorado.

Bruce drove up into the mountains, found a suitable campsite area and there was no snow anywhere. We set up our campsite and went to bed. During the night a snow storm hit us and the heavy snow collapsed our make shift shelter. We fixed up a better support system and had no problems with the snow after that. We spent 5 days hunting without success. So Bruce suggested that we go into the town of Saguache and take a nice hot bath at the hotel there. We all agreed and left the campsite as is and headed for that hotel and a hot bath. I didn't know that we could just pay for the bathtub service if we weren't staying the night there. Bruce said that this hotel was unique and had a room with just several bathtubs, soaps and towels. That hot bath felt great. The very next day while we were eating breakfast at the campsite a couple of elk surprised us. We had been walking all over the hillsides looking for elk and what happened. They came to us. We were successful in getting our elk. The elk meat was split up three ways. My freezer was full of elk meat.

Saguache Independence Hotel & Saloon

Our shelter and campsite

Having a few whiskey drinks before going to bed

At work I was called into our commanding officer's office. He said it was my right to have a full blown retirement ceremony. I told him I had been at a couple of these ceremonies and I didn't want anyone to put up with it. I did not want a ceremony. He understood and thanked me for my 26 years of service. But my co-workers wanted to give me a retirement party at a local bar in Denver. That was ok with me.

The first week of January 1991 we had our household goods put into storage pending my final destination. I really didn't know at that time where I wanted to retire at. We drove to San Antonio and stayed there for a couple of months with friends and relatives. I then told my wife that I wanted to retire in Washington State. She said she would give it a try but she really wanted me to retire in San Antonio. We are still in Washington State.

So to all: This 1/2 of One Percent Airman had one hell of a ride over a 26 year period in the Air Force. I have been to many Air Force reunions since I retired and will continue to attend as many as I can because I really look forward to reminiscing with my old comrades in Arms.

CPSIA information can be obtained
at www.ICGtesting.com
Printed in the USA
FSOW04n0604211215
14493FS